Along
Montana & Idaho's
Continental Divide Trail

Photography by Leland Howard
Text by Lynna Howard

WESTCLIFFE PUBLISHERS

www.westcliffepublishers.com

CONTENTS

ACKNOWLEDGMENTS

This book is dedicated to our father and mother, Calvin and Edna Howard, who set for us an example of self-reliance that we failed to live up to—but they love us anyway.

On a personal note, I would like to thank my brother, Leland. I could not have hiked the trail without him. Another photographer would have hiked to a few scenic points along the trail and called it good, but Leland hiked the whole trail. And I would have gotten lost even more often without him.

—Lynna Howard

Many thanks to the Forest Service, National Park, and Bureau of Land Management employees in Idaho and Montana who took time out of their busy schedules to go over the trail route with us.

The following companies generously supplied gear or offered discounts for our expedition:

REI	Sweetwater	CLIF™ BAR
JanSport	U-DIG-IT	Atwater Carey
LowePro	Trails Illustrated	Vasque

Special thanks to the Continental Divide Trail Alliance and Westcliffe Publishers for believing in our ability to get the job done. Part of the proceeds from the sale of this book benefits the Continental Divide Trail Alliance.

International Standard Book Number: 1-56579-343-9
Text Copyright: Lynna Howard, 2000. All rights reserved.
Photography Copyright: Leland Howard, 2000. All rights reserved.

Editor: Jenna Samelson
Designer: Pauline Brown
Production Manager: Craig Keyzer
Map Design: Carol Pando

Published by:
Westcliffe Publishers, Inc.
P.O. Box 1261
Englewood, CO 80150
www.westcliffepublishers.com

Printed in Hong Kong through World Print, Ltd.

Library of Congress Cataloging-in-Publication Data:
Howard, Leland, 1953-
    Along Montana & Idaho's Continental Divide Trail / photography by Leland Howard ; text by Lynna Howard.
        p. cm
        ISBN 1-56579-343-9
        1. Continental Divide National Scenic Trail. 2. Continental Divide National Scenic Trail—Pictorial works. 3. Hiking—Continental Divide National Scenic Trail. 4. Howard, Leland, 1953—Journeys—Continental Divide National Scenic Trail. 5. Howard, Lynna Prue—Journeys—Continental Divide National Scenic Trail. I. Title: Along Montana and Idaho's Continental Divide Trail. II. Howard, Lynna Prue. III. Title.

F721 .H8 2000
917.86—dc21   00-020691

For more information about other fine books and calendars from Westcliffe Publishers, please contact your local bookstore, call us at 1-800-523-3692, write for our free color catalog, or visit us on the Web at **www.westcliffepublishers.com**.

First Frontispiece: *Bearhat Mountain towers over the wet tundra around Logan Pass. At this northerly altitude, the treeline is at about 6,000 feet.*

Second Frontispiece: *Sunrise and low-lying clouds in the Boulder Mountains paint a picture worthy of a master watercolorist.*

Third Frontispiece: *The author and hiking companion, Tempest the German shepherd, pause above Rainbow Lake in the Anaconda-Pintler Wilderness.*

Opposite: *At Little Lake in the Beaverhead Mountains, springtime doesn't come until the first week of August when Lewis' monkeyflowers line the banks of the inlet stream.*

PREFACE

The Montana/Idaho section of the Continental Divide Trail (CDT) presents unique challenges to a photographer. The Continental Divide is the backbone of the Rocky Mountains, which means that the trail itself is often on the highest windswept ridges. Combine this with the short window of hiking weather in the mountains of the Northwest, and I was set for an adventuresome undertaking.

As expected, access also proved to be a problem. Returning to an area several times to capture a good image meant lots of driving, and even more hiking on approach routes. I gained an intimate familiarity with the Continental Divide, and with every rough dirt road that promised even a resemblance of access. I also discovered where the good latté and hamburger shops are in places like Augusta, Montana, and Salmon, Idaho. This may not seem like high-priority information, but to a backpacker this knowledge takes on special significance.

I like the freedom inherent in backpacking. I can stop where I feel I need to in order to get the best images. I've gone on a few expeditions

Fall color brightens the approach to the saddle on the southern flanks of Crown Mountain on the border of the Scapegoat Wilderness.

with outfitters and found it a frustrating experience. Other than the occasional character shot of a cowboy outfitter, I could seldom get the images I wanted. It was like a painter being given all the paint he needs but denied a canvas. My so-called "photographic opportunities" were limited by the needs of the pack animals. If I stopped for more than 20 minutes, the whole expedition was thrown off schedule. Plenty of grass for the pack animals and a short day of riding did not equal plenty of photo opportunities for me.

It would take a very special relationship between an outfitter, or any other traveling companions, and an artist in order to make a successful expedition. There is an undeniable force in me that drives me to do what it takes to get the images I want. My sister will usually put up with this, but most people can't or won't. So I go my own way, often alone. I created many of the images you see in this book after first hiking the CDT with companions, taking a mental note of an area, and then returning alone to capture what I wanted on film.

Hiking all of the Montana/Idaho portion of the CDT provided opportunities I would not have had if I'd just sampled each section. But it also had drawbacks. The hiking season was so short, and we had so many miles to cover that I often couldn't afford to linger in a photogenic spot. Just surviving and finding drinking water sometimes took precedence over seeking the best shots. I could have devoted five years to photographing Montana and Idaho's Continental Divide and still not have done it justice.

When backpacking I carry a medium-format camera even though this means more weight. My style favors this format. A five-pound tripod is adequate for stabilization, especially if I don't extend the legs. I keep everything as simple as possible, whether it's my camera equipment or camping gear. This saves weight and time. I'm not in a hurry when I'm in the mountains, but I don't want to be fiddling with poorly designed camping gear during favorable evening light. Having the right gear becomes far more critical in severe weather.

Sunrise colors Upper Seymour Lake in the Anaconda-Pintler Wilderness.

Long-distance hikers will encounter bad weather—you can bet on that—and I make a point of staying out in difficult conditions because they often result in the most dramatic photographs.

I usually carry only one lens when I'm backpacking. If I have previously scouted out an area, I'll have developed an idea of what I want to capture, and that helps me decide what lens to bring along. Also, by restricting myself to one lens, I find myself more engaged in the creative process. Sometimes a limitation is just the challenge I need to compose a better shot. Of course, carrying less weight is an added benefit that any backpacker can appreciate.

After working so long and hard on this project, I developed a certain affinity for the CDT. I hope you find inspiration in these pages, whether you hike the trail or not. If you decide to go for it, go prepared. Most of the Continental Divide remains truly wild.

—*Leland Howard*

INTRODUCTION

"Is it in the Rocky Mountains?" That's what my friend, Dee, asked when she heard that my brother and I were going to hike part of the Continental Divide Trail (CDT). Dee lives in Iowa, surrounded by cornfields, and thinks that hiking is okay if you end up at a five-star hotel when the sun sets.

"Well…uh, yeah, it's in the Rocky Mountains, but that's kind of like saying that Iowa is in the Midwest. Technically correct—but all the locals would laugh at you." Later, when Leland and I had trouble finding the trail and were looking at maps as if they might speak up and give us a clue, we'd say, "It's in the Rocky Mountains."

Actually, the CDT is also in valleys, on dirt roads, along ridges where there is no trail, next to highways, a hundred miles from the nearest town, and sometimes it is smack dab on the geographical Continental Divide in the thick band of mountain ranges that make up the Rockies.

Starting in the south and walking north, your feet, your eyes, your ears, and your heart will become intimately acquainted with certain

The author takes a break on the crest of the Continental Divide north of Big Hole Pass, on the Montana/Idaho border.

places when you hike the Idaho and Montana segment of the Continental Divide Trail. Among them are:

Henrys Lake Mountains

Centennial Mountains

Beaverhead Mountains
 of the Bitterroot Range

Anaconda Range

Anaconda-Pintler Wilderness

Fleecer Mountains

Highland Mountains

Boulder Mountains

Scapegoat Wilderness

Bob Marshall Wilderness

Lewis and Clark Range

Glacier National Park

And that's just the terrain you'll cover step by step. Wave upon wave of the rugged crests of other mountain ranges rise into view. The Grand Tetons in Wyoming, Idaho's Lemhi Range, and the Bitterroot Range in northern Montana form just a few of the mighty backdrops to the 50-mile view from the crest of the Divide. Near Roger's Pass and the southern border of the Scapegoat Wilderness, we came upon a sign that simply said "Rocky Mountains." Dee was right.

Every knob and knoll in the eastern states is named, but along the Montana/Idaho Continental Divide, one sometimes has to make do with generalities. You'll find yourself standing on top of a significant chunk of sky-hugging terrain, but a search of the topographic map reveals nothing. You are lucky if there's an elevation tag. We thought we'd name all the unanointed promontories "Howard Peak" but had to give up on that idea after racking up more than a dozen Howard Peaks in the first 500 miles. There's something wonderfully free about hiking over nameless terrain, land that bears the touch of humankind so lightly that not even the burden of a name alters its character.

This book is not a guidebook. It doesn't tell you that 6.7 miles west of Aldous Lake the trail climbs from the Idaho side to the crest of the Divide and joins Montana's Tipton/Winslow Trail. Well, I guess

Near Pigeon Creek Ridge the interim CDT route follows Fish Creek through the Deerlodge National Forest.

it does now, but for any more guidance of that kind, you'll need the companion to this book, *Montana and Idaho's Continental Divide Trail: The Official Guide.*

In other ways, this book gives you more than a guidebook can deliver—a vicarious experience of actually hiking the trail. Reading the text and seeing the variety of landscapes represented in the photos is an excellent way to scout out and choose a segment of the trail for a shorter excursion.

If you are tough enough to hike hundreds of miles in a single season, this book will help you prepare for that adventure. If you just want us to take your imagination by the hand, please install a seat belt on your recliner before proceeding.

Oh, and by the way, Dee, there are a couple of very nice hotels in Glacier National Park. You have to hike only 941 miles to get there. *The truth arrives slowly, at walking speed.*

—*Lynna Howard*

Next page: *Looking over our shoulders to see how far we've come, we see the Beaverhead Mountains of the Bitterroot Range stretched out behind us.*

11

WESTERN BORDER OF YELLOWSTONE NATIONAL PARK TO INTERSTATE 15

Western Border of Yellowstone National Park to Targhee Pass: Island Park, Moose Creek Plateau, and Henrys Lake Mountains, 35.6 miles

I am famous for getting my brother, Leland, and I into deep trouble. This time I broke all previous records. I signed us up to hike the Montana and Idaho portion of the Continental Divide National Scenic Trail, or Continental Divide Trail, with me writing and Leland taking photos for a guidebook. We were given a mileage estimate of 781 miles, which we didn't know was 200 miles short of the truth. The longest distance we'd ever hiked in one stretch was 55 miles. No sweat.

We looked the trail up on various Forest Service maps. Mysteriously, it seemed to appear and disappear. Well, why would you need a guidebook if it were easy? We have, I told myself and my amused parents, mucho experience in the wilds of the Wild West, and we will find this "primitive trail" and chronicle its every twist and turn. I was excited and too ignorant to be worried.

Leland and I drove to the western border of Yellowstone National Park, near the confluence of the Montana, Idaho, and Wyoming borders. We had maps in hand that clearly showed the Continental Divide Trail (CDT) marching across

The photographer's tent is staked to withstand high winds on an exposed ridge near the trail.

Island Park in the Targhee National Forest. Winter was fast approaching, but we wanted to hike an "easy" section of the trail just to see what it was like, as a shakedown cruise for planning next season's expedition.

The more we drove around looking for a trailhead, the more a sense of impending doom descended. The sky was heavy with great, bruised clouds waiting to dump the first snowfall of the season. From above, I heard a voice and it said, "In the Beginning… There Was No Place to Begin." Solemnly, I repeated this to my brother. We laughed the wild-eyed laughter of those who don't know any better.

There was no trailhead. All the cute little CDT symbols on the map did not exist on the ground. But you know, it was a good thing because the true character of the CDT revealed itself to us at the beginning. We cast our illusions aside and began the meticulous, slow, bulldog-like search for the trail that would be our lot for so many miles under many moons. (Since we hiked the trail, lots of CDT signs have been put up, but when this book went to press, there was still no trailhead in Island Park.)

In this section of the Targhee National Forest, many of the roads have been blocked by the Forest Service and are now trails. The closest one can get to the southern terminus of the

Arrowleaf balsamroot blooms in open meadows along the Continental Divide Trail in the Island Park area of Idaho.

Montana/Idaho CDT is about 2.7 miles west of the Yellowstone National Park boundary line. We finally figured out the best approach and got on the trail.

Frankly, this part of the trail was boring for long stretches. I know I'm not supposed to say that. Okay, if you've never been out of Kansas City, this section of the trail is heart-stopping, breathtaking, a wonder—really. We walked on a black, graveled trode (this is what we call a trail that used to be a road) suitable for cars and trucks but limited to snowmobiles in the winter and to hikers and mountain bikers in the summer. Old logging clear cuts gave Leland his only opportunity for photos from the trail. Spindly, closely spaced lodgepole pines closed off most of the views. The approach routes to finding the trail offered more charming scenery. It was difficult to find a place to camp, and water was scarce.

Occasional clear cuts did offer views of the Centennial Mountains to the west, and of Yellowstone National Park to the east. Also on the positive side, we saw three moose and did not, thankfully, see any grizzly bears. We were briefly entertained by a huge black bear that resembled Orson Welles. This bear ran from us, churning up a cloud of old ash and dust, his bulk not deterring him in the least. Man, was he fast! I thought, "Oh yeah, that's what they're supposed to do. They run from humans." As it turned out, that black bear was one of the few, the proud, and the swift. Most of the bears we were later to meet on the Continental Divide Trail stood their ground or pressured us off the trail.

Island Park is the only portion of the Montana/Idaho CDT that has speed limits, but I guess the bear couldn't read. When hiking, do not exceed the 45 MPH speed limit, or the 25 MPH limit in the steep sections. Winter recreation is a big industry in Island Park and hundreds of miles of snowmobile trails crisscross the terrain. Trail markers and signs for snowmobilers tower 20 feet high, giving one a graphic idea of the depth of the winter snows. What this means to hikers is that the snow doesn't completely melt until mid-July, though it is possible to hike the trails earlier if you don't mind crossing packed snowfields. The trails are wide and gentle, with very little summer traffic, and you need a snowmobile map to find them all. There are lots of intersections, lots of turns and wanderings back and forth across the Divide. Hello, Idaho. Hello, Montana.

Most of the watercourses shown on the topographic maps are now dry, in part because of the 1988 fires. It was here, about 50 feet off the CDT, that a firewood cutter started the North Fork fires with a cigarette. Yellowstone burned like it had been fire-bombed. Smoke and news journalists swirled around the place for months.

The only 360-degree view in this section is from "Two Top." Here the trail tops out at 8,208 feet in an alpine meadow festooned with all manner of signs and maps, but not, when we were there, a Continental Divide Trail sign. From Two Top we guessed correctly about the route of the CDT and headed downhill toward Highway 20.

Winter sunrise silhouettes lodgepole pines on the Continental Divide near Black Canyon Loop Road in Idaho.

Fresh snow covers the Henrys Lake Mountains in the Gallatin National Forest.

Leland and I talked to a fellow hiker who said his parents wanted to walk the grizzly corridor from Yellowstone to Canada because they'd heard there were no roads, that they would be hiking in wilderness all the way. I guess they planned to close their eyes and levitate over Highway 20 and dozens of other paved and dirt roads that run east and west across the corridor. A hiker can find solitude in a lot of places, but civilization also makes a brash appearance now and again.

At 35.6 miles from the Yellowstone Park border, the CDT crosses Highway 20 at Targhee Pass and starts seriously climbing again. Targhee Pass (pronounced TAR-gee, with a hard "g") bears the name of a Bannock Indian warrior killed by the Crow Indians in 1871 or 1872.

After three days of hiking on the snowmobile trails through Island Park, we made for Alice's Restaurant, one mile east along the highway. We knew we would not encounter another restaurant that was this close to the trail until Glacier National Park some 900 miles later, so we took full advantage of the "real," non-backpacking food.

Targhee Pass to Interstate 15:
Henrys Lake and Centennial mountain ranges, 94.5 miles

Shoshone Indians used Targhee Pass as the easiest route to buffalo hunting grounds between the Musselshell and Yellowstone rivers. Now it serves as the easiest route for tourists to enter Yellowstone National Park at the town of West Yellowstone. The two-lane highway sees a lot of traffic, and it seemed more than a little odd to go galumphing across it with our backpacks bouncing.

TIPS REGARDING BEARS

- *Don't smell like food. No fragrances should be used. Carry dried foods.*

- *Don't look like food. If you run from a bear you are acting like prey. Grizzly bears interpret direct eye contact as a challenge, so avert your eyes. Don't shout, but do speak in a soft monotone and back slowly away. Some bears will bluff charge, making a run at you but stopping short of an attack. Don't run from a bluff charge. Some experts say that a predatory black bear, which is usually male, should be treated slightly differently in that shouting or throwing rocks may deter an attack. If a black bear is stalking you, try to hold the high ground.*

- *When you are hiking in bear country, talk loudly, clap your hands, bang your trekking poles together, or sing. Avoid surprising a bear.*

- *Carry pepper spray, and make sure it is oleoresin capsicum spray meant to deter bears. The spray will only work if it is sprayed in the bear's eyes, nose or mouth. If you use the spray incorrectly, it will attract bears. If you get pepper spray on yourself or your gear, wash immediately and/or get out of the backcountry as quickly as possible. Be aware of wind direction before using the spray.*

- *If a bear attacks, use your pepper spray. If the bear does not retreat and knocks you down, lie flat on the ground, with your arms and hands covering your head and neck. Leave your backpack on to protect your back, curl up to protect your stomach, or dig your toes into the ground to keep yourself on your stomach. If the bear rolls you over, keep rolling until your stomach is again covered.*

- *Do not hike alone in bear country.*

- *If you're close enough to photograph a bear, you're too close.*

- *You can do everything right and still have an unwanted encounter with a bear. There are no guarantees.*

Trumpeter swans fly over the Buffalo River as the sun sets in the Island Park Caldera.

ISLAND PARK CALDERA

Island Park is the world's largest recognized caldera, a collapsed volcanic chamber about 18 to 23 miles in diameter, and shaped like an enormous shallow bowl. Roughly half a million years ago, large shield volcanoes erupted in what is now eastern Idaho. The Continental Divide National Scenic Trail traverses the eastern edge of the Island Park Caldera, and the western edge of the Yellowstone Caldera. According to geological records of past eruptions, this area is due to explode again soon. Double bubble, toil and trouble.

TRUMPETER SWANS

Majestic trumpeter swans, North America's largest waterfowl, are permanent residents in Island Park. Fewer than 100 swans were counted in 1935, but now about 500 swans nest in the Greater Yellowstone area, which includes the Red Rock Lakes National Wildlife Refuge in Centennial Valley and the Island Park area. It is a birdwatcher's paradise, and the swans are joined by cranes, woodpeckers, nuthatches, eagles, owls, geese, kinglets, chickadees, and wrens to name just a few. Forty-five species have been counted as permanent residents, and many more migrating and seasonal birds add to the mix.

It may be July, but at 10,000 feet, snowfields still decorate the high ridges near Targhee Peak in the Henrys Lake Mountains.

In October the first snows of the season dust the Lionshead area of the Henrys Lake Mountains.

Under a low sun, the silvery gray trunks of whitebark pines looked like a light inside the bundles of green needles. To see whitebark pines you have to get out of your car and start hiking. They are a sure sign that some serious elevation is being gained. Wind-pruned versions as short as shrubs cling to the highest slopes, and the normally whitish trunks can be polished to a warm blush. On this leg of our expedition, we found 40-foot trees in the lee of the Divide and two-foot krummholz (German for "twisted wood") on the ridge at 10,000 feet.

From Targhee Pass to Mile Creek, the trail crosses a "grizzly bear recovery area," which sounds like AA for bears, but is actually a place where bears that have had too much contact with humans get a second chance. Three strikes and they're out of Yellowstone and transported to a recovery area. Gallatin National Forest rangers have put up warning signs: "There are special orders for food storage within this Grizzly Bear Recovery Area…Human food and beverages, horse food, dog food, either in your possession or left unattended must be kept

Food bags are hung high in a tree in compliance with guidelines for camping in a "Grizzly Bear Recovery Area."

unavailable to Grizzly Bears…Keep a clean camp. Items are considered unavailable if they are stored in a closed, bear resistant container… or suspended at least 10 feet clear of the ground at all points and 4 feet horizontally from any supporting tree or pole. Violation punishable by a fine of $500."

We always carry 25 feet of rope and waterproof food bags. We hang the bags 100 yards away from our tents. When we were there, we did not see any bear sign—paw prints, scratched trees, bear scat—but opted to err on the side of caution.

North of Targhee Pass, we followed old roads, snowmobile trails, and newly cut footpaths to Targhee Divide, a saddle that separates two tributaries of Targhee Creek. The distinctive, resting-lion shape of Lionhead Peak cast its regal gaze upon the trail.

The potential for dramatic photos was excellent. Leland took photos in the fresh snow of October and during the wildflower extravaganza of June and July. Along the way, we were excited to find old, metal survey markers with "Ida" on one side and "Mont" on the other. The Continental Divide forms the border between the states for hundreds of miles, so spotting these markers is very reassuring, especially where the footpath isn't clear.

The Henrys Lake Mountains dominate this segment of the CDT. The small mountain range is shaped like an arch that connects the Centennial Mountains to the Madison Creek and Moose Creek plateaus. The northern Henrys Lake Mountains escaped the 1988 fires, so tall mixed conifers line the trail.

We camped near Targhee Divide, then day-hiked to Edwards Lake, a shallow tarn at 10,500 feet. This is the highest section of the Montana/Idaho Continental Divide that hikers may easily access, and it also provides an awe-inspiring look at the Lee Metcalf Wilderness and the entire length of the Centennial Mountains.

There are 50 switchbacks between Targhee Divide and the Mile Creek trailhead near Highway 87. Yes, I know, it was a bit anal to count switchbacks, but the route of the trail didn't appear correctly on any of the maps, so I drew it on the topo as

The author's tent is visible just below Targhee Peak in the Henrys Lake Mountains.

accurately as I could for the sake of the guidebook. The switchbacks were designed for horse traffic, so they accounted for seven miles of descent, or of climbing, depending on which way one was headed. The elevation change was 3,112 feet. It was only 18.3 miles from Targhee Pass to the Mile Creek trailhead, a perfect car-shuttle hike for beginners who just want to sample a short section of the Continental Divide Trail.

In July, cows grazed near the Mile Creek trailhead, fostering an insanity of flies (worse than a swarm of flies). A local rancher showed up and cheerfully noted that "the flies are the worse I've seen 'em. You're not plannin' on drivin' here are you? 'Cause this road is closed." We assured him that we were innocent backpackers and got the heck out of there as quickly as we could.

In light snow, we covered the section of trail between Highway 87 and Red Rock Pass. This is one of many places where the Continental Divide doubles back on itself, a river of rock with tight meanders. We could see the impressive Centennial Mountain Range for miles as we walked south

This is what passes for July weather in the Centennial Mountains near Red Rock Pass.

along a rolling plateau thick with sagebrush, dotted here and there with pine or aspen forests. The Centennial Mountains run in an east-west line for more than 40 miles, defining the border between Montana and Idaho.

The Centennial Valley, also visible from the trail, holds the Red Rock Lakes National Wildlife Refuge, home to hundreds of trumpeter swans and other aquatic birds. Would-be adventurers can hike this mellow, 12.2-mile section to Red Rock Pass in a single day.

All along the Divide, we found that animals use the human trail as part of their game trail system, and the level path seemed to offer critters a good spot for a midday nap. A moose, crashing through the underbrush south of Antelope Road, got my heart pumping. I thought the nearly black animal was a bear at first, but it mutated into the backside of a moose rapidly decamping.

Moss thrives in a shady forest in the Centennial Mountains.

In October, we camped near Red Rock Pass and by the following morning, a snowstorm had cleared and the landscape was perfect for photography, a real Fairy Snow Queen day, with the rising sun reflecting off millions of ice crystals caught on grasses, sagebrush, and trees.

The following spring, we crossed the road over Red Rock Pass and entered the Centennial Mountains. Hell Roaring Creek, the most distant headwaters of the Missouri River, was about three miles up the trail. The creek's waters end up in the Gulf of Mexico, some 4,200 miles downstream as the kayaker paddles. In the spring and early summer, the creek is deadly deep, swift, and cold. Tempting snow bridges may remain into June, pretty death traps that arch over the water, ready to collapse under a hiker's weight. The Bureau of Land Management plans to build a bridge over the stream. Early-season hikers should detour around the creek crossing, using the Nemesis Mountain Trail a couple of miles west of the pass. Late-season hikers will have no trouble fording the stream—unless you are accompanied by a paranoid llama.

At Red Rock Pass, my brother and I added two llamas to our expedition. This turned out to be a mistake of biblical proportions. Our local rent-a-llama rancher provided us with one experienced beast of burden named Popeye. Popeye carried 70 pounds of gear and waded cautiously through water and bogs. His companion, Pogo, was a lost cause. He jumped everything from running streams to trickles of snowmelt, endangering our gear. We tethered Popeye and spent hours working with Pogo, outfitting him with two lead ropes and coaxing him through puddles. "See, it won't hurt you." When we thought we had made some progress, we proceeded up the trail, only to have Pogo leap another infinitesimal strand of water, knocking Leland down and then trampling him.

Arrowleaf balsamroot fills meadows and aspen groves with color in June and early July. Native Americans used this abundant flower for both medicine and food.

Pogo, now loose, bounded up the trail toward me, his light, 20-pound load bouncing precariously. In a panic I held onto Popeye's lead rope and simultaneously levitated about 10 feet off the trail. I still don't know how I managed it, but at least I avoided being trampled by several hundred pounds of lunatic llama.

True to his social llama nature, Pogo finally fetched up next to Popeye. Disgusted by his cohort's unseemly behavior, Popeye started spitting. Pogo returned fire and I was caught in the middle. Desperation bred a semblance of courage, so I grabbed Pogo's lead rope and held on while Leland came to the rescue. Violent kicking joined the spitting, and Popeye's load ended up under his belly. A llama's belly is very sensitive, so Popeye increased his athletic display. Leland got the load righted with only minor injury to his knee, but let me tell you, those books that say a llama can't kick hard enough

Arrowleaf balsamroot, Indian paintbrush, and other wildflowers bloom on a ridge above Blair Lake in the Centennial Mountains.

to hurt you are dead wrong. We separated the two beasts and hitched them to trees. Leland said a few things I can't repeat. He checked the camera gear in his day pack and discovered that Pogo had cracked the housing on one of his cameras. He said a few more things that I really can't repeat!

We continued to climb the ridge west of Hell Roaring Canyon, battling deadfall all the way. Freak downbursts the previous winter had snapped the tops off hundreds of trees and felled others, roots and all, across the trail. It was the worst possible situation for pack stock. Popeye was smart enough to duck under the high deadfall and was good at stepping over the low stuff. Pogo walked serenely up to a head-high log and slammed his face right into it. Leland and I just about fell over laughing. It was very good slapstick comedy, but poor trekking technique. Leland eased the llama's head under the obstacle and we went up the trail a few yards, letting Pogo jump the low stuff because we'd given up on modifying that behavior. Pogo then halted and buried his face in a small pine tree. A tiny trickle of snowmelt crossed the trail and Pogo was scared again. We tethered Pogo to Popeye, and Popeye dutifully pulled the recalcitrant young llama up the trail for about two hours. When Popeye had enough of pulling more than his own weight, he lobbed a big wad of green spit onto my hat. We pressed on as best we could, already half a day behind schedule.

"We could see the impressive Centennial Mountain Range for miles as we walked south along a rolling plateau thick with sagebrush, dotted here and there with pine or aspen forests."

We camped at Blair Lake, having made 7.4 miles in eight hours. We got the llamas staked out and the tents set up just before a hailstorm swept over the horizon, paused over the lake, and dumped everything it had. I dove into my tent and recorded the hail on my pocket tape recorder. It sounded like a herd of buffalo pounding over the plains. On the tape, you can hear the hail pummeling the tent and me trying to talk, but laughing so hard that it is almost unintelligible. "This must be [giggle] the romantic part [full-on laughing]." That's a reference to people who have told us that we have a "romantic" job, while hinting that they'd like to come along on an expedition. "This must be the romantic part" has since served us well to describe many situations.

We woke the next day to blustery weather. Through intermittent breaks in the cloud cover, we could see strong winds pushing plumes of snow off the higher ridges. Huge streams of light-struck crystals, flung into the sky, took on the shape of the wind. One stream slowly curved in on itself, forming the shape of a snail shell or the eye of a hurricane. Nemesis Mountain looked like it was in motion, a jaunty aviator with a silk scarf half-a-mile long.

The window in the clouds closed and the cloud base lowered to devour my tent. Socked in, we couldn't have followed even a marked trail, let alone the pitiful excuse for a trail that existed at that time, so we moved the llamas to better forage and hunkered down to wait out the weather. Blair Lake is supposedly famous for fishing opportunities. I couldn't tell you.

The next morning brought clear weather and the chance to leave. The llamas had enjoyed a full day of rest, so I figured they'd be willing. They weren't. After two hours of struggle, we had them saddled and packed. Crayon-bright wildflower displays west of Blair Lake raised our spirits. The trail disappeared, but we found flags marking its future location near explanatory signs for the Sheep Experimental Station. Sheep graze large portions of the Centennials and the signs are a form of rudimentary PR telling us why this is a good thing, but noting that sheep can carry a disease dangerous to pregnant women. As none of us were pregnant, we proceeded.

All was well for about a quarter-mile, until we came to deadfall hell. Downed trees blocked the trail every five to 10 feet. We tethered the llamas and went to look for a detour. We found a route that looked reasonably easy and that would intersect the trail above us.

As we traversed a meadow, with Leland leading the llamas, Pogo dipped his head into the grass to brush off flies and his halter came off. He was too dumb to realize that he was free and kept trekking behind Popeye. In a quiet monotone, I said to Leland, "He's loose. Pogo's loose." Leland said "What?" and didn't stop. Pogo noted his unfettered state and started to drift. I knew that without a corral, we'd never be able to catch him if he decided he didn't want to be caught. I grabbed his neck in a big hug with both arms. Pogo began to fling me

"Through intermittent breaks in the cloud cover, we could see strong winds pushing plumes of snow off the higher ridges. Huge streams of light-struck crystals, flung into the sky, took on the shape of the wind."

around the meadow like a sack of potatoes. Leland was now fully cognizant of the problem. Leading Popeye, he came around to the rescue, fetching Pogo's halter with his free hand. Popeye did not like being in close proximity to the flying sack of potatoes, so another spitting and kicking scene erupted. It's really a shame that no one was there to capture the comedy on video. We were all bug-eyed: me, Leland, and the llamas.

There was nothing to do but go on. We intersected the cut trail on an alpine ridge and kept climbing. The trail disappeared again, but survey flags led us uphill and across some snowfields for views of the vertical, north-facing cliffs on the Montana side of the Divide. I walked shallow switchbacks for the llamas, leading a willing Popeye while Leland tugged and coaxed Pogo up the mountain.

Coming down from Taylor Mountain, we struck an old mining road. Pogo seemed to resort to sleepwalking, so we stopped to let the llamas rest; then couldn't get them going. Once again, we had barely covered seven miles. There was no water and no place to camp. With superhuman effort we got the caravan on the move and covered another four miles, all of it downhill, before we stopped for the night.

"Overcome the desire for comfort."
—U.S. Army Survival Manual FM21-76

Early October hits Red Rock Pass. The Centennial Mountains, which form the Montana/Idaho border for more than 40 miles, loom in the distance.

Acid yellow and rust-orange lichen adorns rocks on the Continental Divide north of Red Rock Pass in the Henrys Lake Mountains.

Now a day-and-a-half behind schedule, we began to realize that there was no way we would be able to meet our support crew at Aldous Lake. I set my tent up quickly and hiked another three miles along the Divide, looking to see what we had to face tomorrow and hoping to see some sign of the support crew. There was no support crew, there were no footprints, and the trail was destined to disappear again…but the elevation changes were mellow, which gave me some hope. On my way back to camp, the setting sun lit the distant Tetons. I walked, utterly alone, along the grassy spine of the Divide, a thickly forested world laid out at my feet.

We were up at first light, knowing we might need all the daylight hours to search for the support crew. Popeye kicked up such a fuss at being saddled that we had to tether not only his neck to a tree but both of his hind legs. As soon as he was saddled he was as polite as could be, resigned to the inevitable, I guess. Pogo had decided to kill us if we came near him. Nevertheless, he lined up behind Popeye because he liked it there; tethered to Popeye's pack saddle, Pogo, too, was suddenly docile and ready to trek. We gingerly packed him up and were on our way.

We made our slapstick way though one last obstacle course of dead-fall. At noon, from a high point on the ridge, we spotted the support crew and the llama trailer in a meadow far below us. Hallelujah! One-half of the support crew was Dad, who has enough wilderness experience to keep worry at bay when we are two days late and 10 miles short. He had looked over the maps, observed the weather, and picked an intermediate spot to meet us. The other half of the support crew was Mom, who judged that we'd be running short of food and had enough fuel ready to stoke a small army of hikers. Mom took a picture of us coming in, and I don't think I've ever seen a more pitiful sight. I have paid her not to publish it.

Since the dark days of our llama wars, I have met hikers who are happy with llamas as pack animals. A family in the Anaconda-Pintler Wilderness epitomized successful llama owners. They trained their animals from birth, hiked about seven miles per day on mellow terrain with good trails, and then set up camp in a place where the llamas could rest while they day-hiked. No doubt there are Rambo llamas that can do better, but I haven't met them.

At the conclusion of the llama debacle, we were not quite halfway through the Centennial Mountains. Transporting llamas and washing llama spit and shit off our gear cost us a week of the short hiking season. When we returned to the trail, our brother, Jerry, and his son, Jesse, joined us. They proved far easier to handle than llamas, and the whole jaunt went off without a hitch. Well, almost without a hitch—we did get lost a couple of times, but it was the kind of lost where we knew where we were, we just couldn't find the trail.

Because we were charged with writing a guidebook, we spent time looking for the real and the proposed routes of the CDT. If you don't care whether or not you're on THE route, it's possible to trek cross-country in the questionable areas and find the trail again where it is clearly marked. Topographic map reading skills are a must, and hikers have to resist being misled into following horse-packing trails that lead down the major drainages. Other visitors ride or hike along watercourses, usually with fishing or hunting destinations in mind. The CDT is clear where it follows these trails, but disappears where it diverges to follow the Divide. The locals cannot understand why anyone would insist on hiking along the Divide when there are plenty of logical routes that reflect good judgment. As we hiked along the Divide, the quixotic nature of our quest became more and more apparent.

With the exception of the area around Aldous Lake, we didn't see any other humans, and we had a great time wandering around on the spacious Divide, looking for the trail. Thanks to our support crew, we had the luxury of carrying only three to four days' worth of food. A lighter pack makes one a lot more willing to backtrack and to explore various routes. Jerry to Jesse: "Our guides are lost again." Twelve-year-old Jesse to Jerry: "What else have you got that I can eat?"

It was July, and we thought we had waited long enough for all the snow to melt, but we still had to cross small snowfields on north-facing slopes. Avalanche danger is intense earlier in the season. In years of normal snowfall, the trail can be impassable in June.

The Forest Service had marked a route with carsonite posts where the trail crosses a meadow on Big Table Mountain. With Jesse's help, we put CD symbols on the posts. Cow elk called to their calves in the background while we put the signs up.

Support crew quote: "If they want to call it a trail, then you ought to be able to find it."

"As we hiked along the Divide, the quixotic nature of our quest became more and more apparent."

There are few access points to the CDT in the Centennial Mountains. Two-wheel-drive cars are limited to the trailheads at Red Rock Pass, Aldous Lake, and Pete Creek Divide. Check the topo maps and you'll see that these trailheads allow you to split the hike into segments of about 30 miles. We met our support crew again at Pete Creek Divide. A great horned owl announced our arrival. We indulged in the luxury of washing up, and resupplied our packs before we headed west again.

On the west edge of Little Table Mountain, wooden CD signs and new blazes led us to what used to be a gate in what used to be a fence. As the signs directed, we made a U-turn and paralleled the fenceline again. We couldn't believe the trail crew had cut and signed such an illogical trail. The fence was no longer a fence and the gate was a ghost of its former self, but, like actors in an absurdist comedy, we hiked to the gate before we crossed the fenceline.

"Howdy, is this the Continental Divide Trail?"

"Oh, yes, you're on it, but you have to go down there to the gate before you can come up here."

"All right then. Have a nice day."

As the trail curved around the southern edge of Little Table Mountain, the unobstructed views reached across Interstate 15 to the Beaverhead Mountains of the Bitterroot Range, the next challenge on the long and winding trail to Canada.

This flower-filled meadow in the Centennial Mountains, a low spot on the Divide west of Aldous Lake, makes a pleasant resting spot.

INTERSTATE 15 TO GOLDSTONE PASS

Southern Beaverhead Mountains of the Bitterroot Range, 145 miles

My brother and I had covered about 130 miles of the trail and were getting used to being the only humans up on the Continental Divide. We'd see a few of our species at a lake or road crossing, then we'd be alone again.

West of Interstate 15, the CDT winds uphill until it reaches the crest of the Divide, from which vantage point one can see forever but probably won't since the only way to make any forward progress is with your head down and the weight of your upper body and pack leaning into the wind. The wind up there pushed against us like the hand of a malevolent god. I struggled to keep from being blown into the valley, where a line camp of the Snowline Cattle Company waited to receive me. The ridge was so narrow in places that it was possible to put one foot in Idaho and one in Montana and look down into both states. From a distance, the ridgeline looked like a deceptively easy hike. Up close, it was a roller coaster of short, but steep, ups and downs. My lungs were going like a set of bellows.

Photographer Leland Howard pauses to survey the view from the Divide.

The gusty winds literally blew me backward several times. Anyone who has carried a fully loaded backpack at high altitudes will appreciate the gravity of the situation. When it came to the Good, the Bad, and the Ugly on the Continental Divide, this was Bad. Leland and I took a break for water and snacks and discussed the situation. The wind blew a tune across the top of my water bottle and siphoned through the sockets of a cow skull. We decided that the CDT gig rated as more extreme than rafting Idaho's Bruneau River. We could have died on the Bruneau, but it would have all been over in three days.

We crossed the border fence where it had been downed by snow and wind and proceeded to sidehill along on the lee side. The lee side was not calm, it was just less buffeted by winds. After hiking a half-mile down the wrong spur ridge, we learned to keep the fence in sight above us. Null and Void (our new hiking monikers—I'm "Null" and Leland's "Void") have been known to lose the trail before, but this mistake was particularly galling.

Sometimes a CDT pole of a distinctive size and height reassured us that we were close to the right route. Would-be long-distance hikers will get a lot of practice at spotting these poles and telling them apart from fenceposts and dead trees. Most of the time, the

Opposite: *Spring snow blankets the Red Conglomerate/Lima Peaks area of the Beaverhead Mountains.*

INTERSTATE 15 TO BANNACK PASS

The Continental Divide Trail follows the Beaverhead Mountains as they meander like a river, and the trail is like a current within that river. We looped back on our route so closely in places that I was reminded of a story in Lewis and Clark's journals where they traveled all day on the Missouri River by boat, only to camp within an hour's walk of their previous day's campsite.

The name "Beaver's Head" appeared in Lewis and Clark's journals in 1805, when their guide, Sacajawea, identified a rock formation on what is today the Beaverhead River. This river is a major tributary of the Missouri, which Lewis and Clark followed upstream during their ambitious expedition to find waterways that might connect to the Columbia River basin and the Pacific Ocean.

The Lima exit of Interstate 15 provides access to Bannack Pass in the Beaverhead Mountains. Lima is the only outpost with a thin veneer of civilization within 40 miles. From Lima, two-wheel-drive gravel roads get you close to the Divide, and extremely rough four-wheel-drive access roads take you all the way there.

poles were placed just far enough apart to be out of visual range. I began to suspect a bit of sadistic humor on the part of the forest rangers. Or maybe they just figured that nobody in their right mind....

The poles, though of recent vintage, had been so blasted by snow and high winds that the merest vestige of a CD symbol remained on them. I don't think this quite qualifies as Bad, since any signpost on the CDT is Good, there being so many places where there are no signs, no trail, and (if you're Null and Void) little hope.

After several miles of steep sidehilling I developed a blister on my downhill foot. This brings me to the Ugly. Blisters are friction burns. They get red, they puff up, they fill with fluid, and one little blister can take over your entire mind and body. Sheer willpower got me to a snowbank from which a little meltwater trickled, and some pine trees offered shelter from the wind. There was no flat place to roll out a sleeping bag, let alone set up a tent, so we resigned ourselves to sleeping on the slant in a stand of trees that still smelled of last season's cows.

Cows can be Good, Bad, or Ugly. This was Ugly. This area around the Divide had been heavily grazed, and the ground was pulverized by cow hooves. Streams had been churned into a mixture of mud and manure. We were up on the Divide before the cows were herded into the high country to munch the spring grass, but damage from the previous season still lingered.

Another side of Ugly, to my mind, is all the damned fences. Some of them are needed for cattle control, but some are boundary markers and, as such, are completely unnecessary. The old survey markers are sufficient. Most of the fences at higher altitudes get blown down anyway. There you are in the middle of nowhere with more mountain ranges than you can count stretching out on all sides and this idiotic barbed wire fence intrudes on the

Mule's ears flourish on Bannack Pass in the Beaverhead Mountains near the Montana/Idaho border.

Spring snows water aspen groves below the Divide in the Beaverhead Mountains.

scene. We followed the fence for 10 miles from Horse Creek to Shineberger Creek.

A bit of wisdom from Chief Joseph of the Nez Percé Indians (1832–1904) crossed my mind: "The country was made without lines of demarcation, and it is no man's business to divide it…"

Before we left the wind-scoured ridge, an eagle crossing from Montana into Idaho didn't see me until the last minute and so passed within 10 feet of my face, right at eye level. A startled look crossed the eagle's face and then it swerved away. The moment definitely qualified as Good. And if it hadn't been for all that wind I wouldn't have had such a close encounter. Good, Bad—depends on your point of view.

Above Shineberger Creek, impassable peaks forced the trail off the Divide. We began a confusing detour through lower terrain. The trail tread repeatedly appeared and disappeared. We found a few blazes in wooded areas, but had to be careful in distinguishing manmade blazes from places where elk and deer had scraped their antlers. Manmade blazes usually look like a lowercase "i," but some trail crews are sloppier than others, and an aging blaze can lose its clarity.

The dot-over-slash style of blazing trees has been used to mark trails since the Lewis and Clark era.

Conundrums such as branded arrows on a post, conflicting with arrows on signs attached to the post, reminded me of a Three Stooges comedy. The high point of this comedy was a combination of sign and post arrows indicating four different directions for the Continental Divide Trail, none of which were correct. In my notes, I resorted to directions like, "keep the Lima Peaks off your right shoulder and stay near the 7600 contour line on the topo map."

Little Beaver Creek, about 23 miles west of I-15, was running high with snowmelt. Leland jumped it successfully and I attempted to. It was a close call, but I didn't make it, slipping back into the stream near the far bank. I managed to keep my pack above water and made a decision to ford all future streams by sedately wading, no matter how cold the water. Throughout our trek, we were more cautious than we would have been on a shorter expedition. We had hundreds of miles and many months of hiking ahead of us. There was no room for injuries, no time-outs for healing.

We camped east of Sawmill Creek, near a tributary stream, where there was an excellent view to the south of "The Thumb," a formation on the Divide that turned reddish gold in the setting sun. Coyotes serenaded us with a

In May and June, snow is common in the higher elevations of the southern Beaverhead Mountains.

long melody of howls and a light breeze stirred a meadow full of yellow "sunray" flowers. My hiking boots were still a little wet, squish, squish, but the rest of me was reasonably dry and happy.

By morning everything was wet. No, it didn't rain on us, but the low meadow, surrounded as it was by streams, developed its own London-like mist and fog as soon as the temperature dropped. Our tents were wet rags, dripping inside and out. We should have known better, we did know better, which only goes to show you how much fatigue can affect your judgment. We looked at the maps and saw that we could cover enough distance to meet our support crew in one day, and a good thing, too. At the time, I didn't realize what a great margin of error the support crew gave us. When we hiked longer distances without them later in the expedition, the threat of hypothermia thanks to wet gear became my own personal nightmare monster.

The Red Conglomerate Peaks were identified by a sign that looked decidedly anachronistic in such an untrammeled place and after so many miles of unsigned trail. We were back on the physical Divide, but at the sign the trail disappeared, which is just perfect when you think about it. For one brief, shining moment, we knew where we were. It's against the nature of the Continental Divide National Scenic Trail to simultaneously tell you where you are and where you should go. That would be an embarrassment of riches. Binoculars would have revealed some clues in the meadow below us: CD posts used by cows to

The Tendoy Mountains form a sunlit backdrop to the CDT near Morrison Lake.

From Bannack (or Medicine Lodge) Pass, the CDT soon begins its turn northward as it follows the line of the Beaverhead Mountains.

scratch an itch, some of them leaning at odd angles. An enormous pile of rocks to the north, Garfield Mountain, dominated the horizon.

We intercepted a jeep track near a tributary of Little Sheep Creek, puzzled over more they-went-that-a-way trail signs, and committed ourselves to a track that had seen more black bears than jeeps in recent years.

We huffed and puffed uphill to Buffalo Spring and then had some fairly easy hiking in open terrain. We met our support crew at Bannack Pass, named for the Bannack Indians, who used the passes across the Continental Divide to access buffalo hunting grounds in what is now Montana. On some maps, this pass is named "Medicine Lodge Pass" in reference to Native American sweat-houses that used to exist along the creek on the Idaho side of the pass. The CDT also crosses the similarly named "Bannock Pass" more than fifty miles to the north. Major confusion can result if hikers fail to distinguish between Bannack and Bannock. As we crossed the pass, rain obscured the valleys below us and light snow coated our gear.

We filled our bellies with home cooking at Mom's Mobile Wilderness Cafe, filled our packs with less desirable food, and got back on the trail. Deadman Lake was our next goal. Starving or dead men have left a

The author pauses to take in the view south of Bannock Pass (north of Bannack Pass), as a storm brews in the distance.

legacy of sharply descriptive names along the Divide—Starvation Gulch, Deadman Pass, Deadhorse Canyon, Thirsty Creek, and Hungry Hill, to name a few. We were always on the lookout for food ourselves. Nicholia Creek promised the best trout fishing that I saw. In the upper reaches, fish swarmed away from my boots when I forded the stream. Scott Peak and Italian Peak loomed over the creek's headwaters, snowcapped and inaccessible.

Near Rock Creek we briefly disturbed some residents on the trail. Next to a survey stake, left by a ranger optimistic about creating a visible trail someday, two spindly elk calves were bedded down. We didn't see them until we'd almost stepped on them, whereupon they broke cover and headed uphill to join their elders. It's a lovely thing to be alone in the backcountry, slowed to walking speed, and seeing with eyes that aren't worn out by computer screens and TV. The elk were feasting on spring-green grasses and no one had told them not to park their babies right on the route of the CDT.

Having seen the best of the details, all we needed was the best of the big picture, and in a saddle at the head of Meadow Creek we got it. Cottonwood Mountain bulked up in the neck-craning vicinity; Idaho's Lemhi Range nicely filled the middle ground; and the highest peak in

Idaho, the 12,655-foot Borah Peak in the Lost River Range, punctuated the horizon. Our range of view was more than 50 miles. This was what we paid for with sweat.

A venturi effect pumped up the wind's velocity as it funneled through the notch in the mountain range. Even in the raucous and churning wind, I was wading in a wide silence as if all words and sentences had been swept from my mind.

It was near Coyote Creek that we watched a herd of elk flowing over the foothills like a brown river. A rain shadow keeps the mountains here drier than other parts of the trail, and the result is that sagebrush steppe dominates the foothills, which makes for good long-distance sightseeing. A thin band of forest stretches out at about 8,000 feet, with alpine meadows or barren rock above. Sheer cliffs rise over the Tex Creek basin, where the stream feeds grassy meadows and thick stands of conifers. Tex Creek

Spring green below contrasts with white above. The aspen trees leaf out in late May, but the conifers above 6,000 feet are frosted with new snow in Beaverhead National Forest.

is a better place to camp than Morrison Lake. The lake is a small gem of water, but a bit overcamped by local fishermen.

As far as photos are concerned, the ridge north of Morrison Lake, with its sinuous curves and long views, is a classic. The trail from Morrison Lake north to Bannock Pass offers the highest average elevation on the Montana/Idaho CDT. However, all that high and wide is dwarfed by Idaho's Lemhi Range, a constant companion to the west that boasts 23 peaks over 10,000 feet. The geographical Continental Divide is not always the highest terrain in sight. In clear weather, we could see 100 miles of the Divide that we had already hiked. Leland burned film like a crazy man.

We met some rangers, green-jeans in green-mobiles. They were on their way to stake out a reroute of the CDT around Elk Mountain. Horse Prairie Peak of Elk Mountain is the highest point on the Montana/Idaho portion of the CDT route and

Buttercups flourish in the Lima Peaks area of the Beaverhead Mountains.

a relatively easy climb. Luckily, we hiked the Elk Mountain section before the new trail was finished so we got to climb two 10,000-foot-plus peaks in one day. Just so we could describe where it goes, we also walked part of the new route, which is basically a couple hundred yards below the old route. I guess the rangers didn't want hikers to turn into lightning rods on the high points. Elk Mountain was not an easy place to find, being a long way from anywhere, and requiring topographic maps for both road access and hiking.

Rangers' remarks in reply to questions about access roads:
    Idaho-based ranger: "Is that in Montana?"
    Montana-based ranger: Is that in Idaho?"

One side of Elk Mountain held a deep pile of snow with a delicate cornice like an eyebrow above it, and wildflowers completely covered the other side. We couldn't walk without stepping on the carpet of miniature forget-me-nots: blue, purple, pink, yellow, and white. It was lovely while the sun was out, and bone-chillingly cold when the sun set. There was no one up there but four mountain goats.

Deadman Pass was on our route as we headed downhill from Elk Mountain to Bannock Pass. One story has it that a scout for the army during the Nez Percé war found a dead man on the pass, but no one could identify the body. Another tale involves a prospector who died when he fell from his horse. Whiskey Spring Creek below the pass was a stopover for freight wagons hauling whiskey from

Coulters lupine blooms in late May and June on the Divide in the Beaverhead Mountains.

Red Rock, Montana, to Salmon, Idaho. I'm betting on the drunken prospector story.

It's only about 28 miles from Bannock Pass to Lemhi Pass, but when we hiked the route, there was no trail between Grizzly Hill and Goat Mountain so the compass and topo maps got a workout. Near Goat Mountain, the trail passed through a gothic graveyard of upended trees whose twisted trunks and bare limbs told the story of a downburst so strong that it must have hit the ridge like a bomb.

Once past Goat Mountain, we intercepted a rough dirt road leading to Lemhi Pass. The road was open to motorized vehicles but seldom used, a statement that can generally apply to most of the roads that serve as trails on the Montana/Idaho CDT. Nine signs marked Lemhi Pass, so we definitely knew where we were. There were signs designating the pass as the Montana/Idaho border, quotes from the Lewis and Clark journals, signs noting the Shoshone Indian hunting trails, more quotes from the journals, Sacajawea Memorial Camp signs, more quotes from the journals, Salmon National Forest boundary signs, and various regulatory signs relating to stock use and motorized vehicles. I never did get used to this phenomenon: On our way to Canada, finding the Continental Divide Trail was a hit-or-miss proposition, but intermittently we'd come upon a place signed like the Times Square of the wilderness.

Lynna Howard makes notes on the trail south of Morrison Lake in the Beaverhead Mountains. The CDT approaches and then bends away from the snowy ridge visible in the background.

Here's what Lewis wrote in his journal about the view from the top:

"August 12, 1805. After refreshing ourselves, we proceeded on to the top of the dividing ridge, from which I discovered immense ranges of high mountains still to the west of us, with their tops partially covered with snow."

Lewis was referring to Idaho's Lemhi Range. What he expected to see was an end to mountain ranges and the beginning of a good waterway to the Columbia River, but the view from Lemhi Pass put a damper on that dream. We hiked down to nearby Sacajawea Memorial Camp to check out the water source.

Another quote from Lewis' journal:
"Judge then of the pleasure I felt in allaying my thirst with this pure and ice cold water. Here I halted a few minutes and rested myself."

Along the Continental Divide, the past presses up against the present. You can pick up the past in your hands, you can feel it in the wind; Meriwether Lewis' words, Indian arrowheads and Indian sorrows, miner's tools, and buffalo jumps. On the Divide, history is raw. There is the feeling that if you turn aside from whatever rough track you are on,

you will walk back in time. Like the pioneer's campfire, your flashlight will be the only light in a great swale of darkness.

We pitched our tents and, in my dreams, I hiked over mountains stacked up like clouds in the sky. In the early morning light, grasses in the meadow were beaten gold. Their pale expanse was like a carpet, shaken to release its light. The carpet of grass ran north into a stand of trees. We packed up and followed the golden path.

Mountains that are seen at a distance are usually blue, but on this day the blue was more profound—a drenching, eye-calming blue. We lost the sun to a thin layer of clouds, but would have lost it anyway to tree shadows. Above the Kitty Creek and Eunice Creek drainages, we entered the glimmering gloom that is characteristic of dense lodgepole pine forests. A ranger we spoke to said that he once spent three hours "wandering around in Montana" looking for the CDT here. The tree blazes are critical. Lose sight of them and you can get lost 10 feet from the so-called trail.

About 10 miles north of Lemhi Pass, the CDT enters a different kind of puzzle, a rat's nest of dirt roads, tracks, and snowmobile trails. Sometimes the CDT follows one of these for a short distance; often it crosses them. I stopped counting after about twenty intersections, convergences, and divergences. We followed the blazes like they were holy. Here was an opportunity to get lost on roads instead of in a trackless forest.

At last, the trail broke free and climbed onto a rocky ridge. The views into Montana's Big Hole Valley were sweet, and there was only one unambiguous ridge to follow all the way to Goldstone Pass.

Alpine forget-me-nots and other wildflowers blossom above 9,000 feet on the Continental Divide.

Previous page: A midday storm builds on a windswept ridge of the Continental Divide north of Morrison Lake in the Beaverhead Mountains.

The winter sun highlights Lemhi Pass on the Continental Divide, near Sacajawea Memorial Spring.

GOLDSTONE PASS TO CHIEF JOSEPH PASS

—————— ♥▲▼ ——————

Beaverhead Mountains of the Bitterroot Range, 76.1 miles

Snow, snow, and more snow. On July 4th we explored the trail from both Idaho and Montana, approaching from several angles before we were convinced that the depth of the snow and the avalanche danger added up to suicide for hikers. Great views abounded though—enough to stop your heart with the wild beauty of snow, ice, and rock. With all of this heart-stopping, breathtaking, mind-boggling scenery, one faces considerable physical danger just looking at the Continental Divide.

In August of the following year, we returned to this section of the trail, which frames the western edge of Montana's Big Hole Valley. As if we had at last paid all our dues, the weather gods blessed us with sunny, warm days. At the highest elevations, snowfields came down to the trail and then politely ended in scalloped, melting edges.

Leland and I had already hiked more than 800 miles when we arrived back at this, our last section of trail. We figured that nothing could surprise us; in fact, we were a bit jaded. Cowbone Lake just wasn't pretty enough

The author relaxes in a meadow above Little Lake as Homer Youngs Peak catches the afternoon light in the Beaverhead Mountains of the Bitterroot Range.

for us. Ho Hum. Part of the trail was not signed, other portions were. Same old story. There was a bewildering array of current and proposed routes. Ask me if we were surprised. The proposed routes led to entertaining dead ends like bogs in Berry Meadows and vertical cliff faces above Pioneer Lake, places where only nature photographers would dare to tread.

Future trail construction will take a more direct path, but when we hiked it, the trail zigzagged up and down several creek drainages, taking us down to the Big Hole Valley before we climbed toward the Divide again. The good thing about this was that the creeks were beautiful, full of fish, and graced with wildflowers. The down side was that we hiked a lot more miles than strictly necessary by taking all the scenic detours.

In the year of the great and lingering snows, we had hiked along the crest of the Divide above Cowbone and Jahnke lakes. High winds had swept the crest clear of snow, but the trail below us was buried to the treetops. The Forest Service's 1989 proposal showed this higher terrain as the preferred route. We did find a lone, weathered CD sign that looked like it had been erected by prehistoric rangers. From Goldstone Pass, we made our way happily

Opposite: A pond on the approach route to Goldstone Pass reflects the evening light.

northward for a few miles, reassured by this lone sign that the CDT trail was on the crest, but then serious trouble began. No trail was cut to get one down again on the Montana side, and tempting ridges leading northwest would only take us into never-never land in Idaho. Class IV climbing with our backpacks on led to Pioneer Lake, a descent possible in August, after the snow has melted.

We followed the interim CDT to Cowbone Lake and then along Darkhorse Creek Road as it plunged toward the valley. A herd of cows fell through the ice on Cowbone Lake and the watery grave, now the resting place of the ivory-colored bones, gave the lake its name.

The roads up every drainage are artifacts from the mining era, leading to prospect holes, abandoned mines, and yellow pine buildings aging into beauty under the high-altitude sun. Most of the roads are too rough to drive, even for jeep jockeys, so they make good trails for people, horses, and mountain bikes.

Glacier lilies appear as soon as the snow melts, sometimes even blooming at the edge of snowfields. This wild garden flowers near Cowbone Lake in the Beaverhead Mountains of the Bitterroot Range.

We made our way along footpaths and roads past the Jahnke Creek drainage, Pioneer Creek, and Berry Meadows. The interim route roughly followed Overland Trail #36, which was fairly well-marked on the Forest Service map, though erratically signed on the ground. The Continental Divide Trail appeared and disappeared on the Forest Service map. On the ground, it was sometimes obvious and sometimes a ghost of an idea of a trail. An attempt to find another section of proposed trail led us to a grassy bog that housed so many elk that it smelled like a cow pasture.

From Berry Creek to Hamby Creek the trail was dim, with occasional blazes leading us over deadfall and through pathless meadows. We saw a couple of beat-up-looking hikers resting near Berry Creek. They looked like victims of a terrible forced march and had no smiles or greetings for anyone.

If you climb the ridges above Cowbone and Jahnke lakes, it is possible to walk the Divide for a couple of miles in both directions. Pictured here is the ridge north of Jahnke Lake.

Continental Divide trekkers hike above and along Montana's Big Hole Valley, "the land of 10,000 haystacks." The valley was the site of a clash between Nez Percé Indians and U.S. troops in 1877, and is now home to some of the richest ranch land in Montana.

THE HOLE-Y LAND

In the West, a "hole" is an open valley, usually a high plateau, surrounded by mountains. Jackson Hole in Wyoming and the Big Hole Valley in Montana are good examples. The term goes back to mountain men and trappers who dropped down out of the mountains into a "hole" for easier travel, and for hunting and fishing expeditions. Montana's Big Hole Valley is 50 miles long, 15 to 20 miles wide, and above 6,000 feet in elevation. A cold, forbidding landscape buried in snow during the winter months, it turns into a paradise of grasslands and clear-running rivers in the summer.

We were still happy campers and became downright jovial at the Hamby Creek and Miner Lake Trail intersection. The trail sign said "Hamby Creek" and its number, 203, matched the number on the Forest Service map. There were even wooden CD signs on adjacent trees. Wow. The trail, a long-since closed road, was good all the way to Rock Island Lakes. We saw a few horsemen and day hikers on this section.

We passed the trail leading to Upper Miner Lakes (a favorite with fishermen), left the last day hikers behind at Rock Island Lakes, and began a steep climb to Little Lake. The switchbacks leading over the saddle were not regulation grade; in fact they were so steep in places that we were almost reduced to using our hands—torture for all concerned, but especially bad for pack stock. The silver lining was that this steep climb, and the fact that it was snowed in most of the year, stopped most of the human traffic.

I hesitate to use the word "pristine." Overuse has stripped the word of all meaning and, let's face it, all along the Divide some human had walked before us. Though we saw few hikers, the traces of human traffic were there. How about this: Little Lake was as close to pristine as we were going to get. The lake was only five miles from Miner Lake Trailhead, but protected as if walls had been built around it, courtesy of the hand of nature. The area above and north of Little Lake was the most glacier-carved terrain that we saw in the Beaverhead Mountains.

Leland was in photographer heaven, so the only model who is ever available in these out-of-the-way spots, yours truly, had the tough job of sitting still for his four-second exposures. I propped my feet up and perused the view, enjoying the enforced leisure. Sometimes life is really rough. Far above us, the mountain goats cropped the jewel-colored grass, oblivious to our intrusion. Fish jumped in the

The Beaverhead Mountains of the Bitterroot Range are silhouetted against the setting sun.

The Twin Lakes outlet stream flows near the Twin Lakes campground at the foot of the Beaverhead Mountains.

lake, snapping at insects with increasing fervor as the evening came to a close. Mosquitoes also grew more active, and my modeling job became a trial and a tribulation. A thunderstorm rolled in over the Divide so we dove into our tents until it passed, giving me some respite from the mosquitoes.

Leland took more photos in the morning light and then we packed up to leave, though we would have preferred to stay another day. One of my beefs about long-distance trekking is that there is seldom time or food enough to linger anywhere. The trail was marked with stone cairns as it continued northward from Little Lake, and then the cairns were no more and tread disappeared in meadows and braided streams of snowmelt.

For a couple of miles, we crossed more spectacular alpine zones. One more steep dive off the Divide led us to Big Swamp Creek and a jeep trail to Ajax Lake. The waterfalls in the Ajax Lake outlet stream jumped downhill in frothy abandon, but the lake itself, a short detour off the CDT, was a disappointment since part of its shoreline had burned. The trail contours across lower terrain near Lena Lake. We followed the newly-cut tread and new signs branded with "CDNST." A few bad apples in the local population have exercised equal opportunity disdain for all signs by blasting them full of bullet holes or tearing them down.

A good, easy-to-find trail led us past Slag-a-Melt Lakes (now there's a mining-era name if I ever heard one) to a saddle on the shoulder of Squaw Mountain. There is an intimidating view from

Big Swamp Creek, above the CDT, flows from Ajax Lake in the Beaverhead Mountains.

Looking east toward the Continental Divide, Montana's Upper Miner Lakes sit just on the other side of these snow-dusted peaks.

this saddle if you are headed north. The highest peaks of the Anaconda Range form the edge of the visible world to the northeast. From this perspective, they don't look like anything a hiker would want to traverse.

From the saddle, we hiked down into a basin full of Douglas-fir trees, some of them sinking gnarled, old-growth roots into the boggy mountainside. Every forest has an individual character.

"From the windy saddle, we slid into the quiet under the trees, then we climbed out again."

This one had an ancient, moss-draped feel, and the air was musty, seldom moved by the winds that raked over the treetops. From the windy saddle, we slid into the quiet under the trees, then we climbed out again. We always had some misgivings about hiking downhill—we knew that for every step down, there would be a step uphill to gain the Divide once more.

On the Divide we found "CDNST" and "Twin Lakes" signs. The lakes and the adjacent improved campground are good access points for the CDT if hikers don't mind some cross-country work through scattered trees to reach the Divide. Twin Lakes used to be on the route of the CDT until new trail was cut near the crest of the Divide.

We followed visible tread northward, cruising along below the Divide to an unnamed lake still necklaced with snow, where we

Before new trail was cut three miles west of Twin Lakes, the CDT route passed through this area. Spur trails still make Twin Lakes a good access point for the Continental Divide Trail.

The shallow inlet to Little Lake in the Beaverhead Mountains is not shown on the topo maps, but it runs all season and is bordered with Lewis' monkeyflowers and lupine well into August.

LEWIS' MONKEYFLOWERS

Lewis' monkeyflowers lined the banks of the inlet to Little Lake in a swath of shocking pink. Mimulus lewisii *is a snapdragon-like plant with blooms that mimic a monkey's face.* Lewisii *refers to Captain Meriwether Lewis, who left his name on everything from entire mountain ranges to these delicate flowers. Apparently, the plant is not good forage for deer, elk, or sheep, but Native Americans ate it both raw and cooked. The leaves are edible as salad greens, and the deep pink to red flowers attract hummingbirds in summer. The double row of flowers lining the streambanks provided a perfect "beauty line" for a photograph of Homer Youngs Peak at the foot of the lake, a pyramid that looks at its own reflection in Little Lake's waters.*

A multitude of small waterfalls cascades from the glaciated cliffs above Little Lake in the Beaverhead Mountains.

A thin coating of ice forms on Twin Lakes in early October.

"We followed visible tread northward, cruising along below the Divide to an unnamed lake still necklaced with snow, where we camped for the night."

camped for the night. Elk skittered away from us into the trees, breaking branches as they went. In the morning, we met another hiker on the trail. Using his watch, he timed his conversation with us and bemoaned the fact that he exceeded his allowed break time. He was also worried about his "fuel." It took me a minute to realize that he was talking about food, not stove fuel. I wondered what he did for a living and guessed "accountant."

We entered Idaho at a saddle above Fourth of July Creek. A narrow spur ridge with a top-of-the-world feel took us across talus slopes on the freeway version of trail construction—rock retaining walls and solid footing on a wide path. The temperature in Idaho was at least 10 degrees warmer and the snow long gone. We wandered back and forth across creeks and climbed up Bradley Gulch to intercept a jeep track on the Montana/Idaho border.

On the Montana side of Morgan Mountain, we climbed over a locked gate and continued on a footpath. Locked gates like this one are likely to unhinge hikers not familiar with primitive trails in the American West. The gates are meant to stop vehicular traffic, not hikers—but sometimes there are no signs to tell you that, and there are no walkarounds or stiles. If a gate is locked, but does not have a "No Trespassing" or "Private Property" sign, hikers are supposed to climb over it. If the gate is not locked, it's meant to stop cattle, and hikers should be sure to close the gate after passing through. It would be helpful if there were Continental Divide Trail directional signs on the gates.

An early snow dusts the photographer's tent in the Beaverhead Mountains of the Bitterroot Range.

The footpath beyond the gate led to a jeep road, where we hiked to Big Hole Pass and crossed the access road coming up from Gibbonsville, Idaho. At lower elevations, the access road was flanked by ponderosa pines, their characteristic red-orange, armorplated trunks and park-like groves a visual delight. The road cut a hole in the forest canopy, and a host of wildflowers flourished in the warm sunlight.

From Big Hole Pass to Chief Joseph Pass, we hiked on four-wheel-drive tracks, footpaths, and cross-country ski trails. The ridge of the Divide was so narrow that we could see into Montana's Big Hole Valley, and into Idaho's Valley of the North Fork of the Salmon River. A sign that simply said "Water" took us on a short detour to an outfitters' camp. The camp was a mess, sprouting rotting hunks of foam, plastic utensils, and

A profusion of wildflowers blossoms in a high meadow near the West Fork of Wimpey Creek drainage.

other debris. Hunting camps like this one look better when they're covered with snow, which is how the hunters see them, and it's one reason for their failure to pack out all their trash. Stuff gets buried under fresh snowfall so they leave it behind. For us, it was quite a disgusting sight, but we just could not pass up the water source since it was the only one available.

We got back on the trail, and glacier lilies sprouting at the edges of melting snow-drifts erased the hunter's debris from my mind. Leland took a few photos and had set up for more when a hailstorm rolled in. We scurried for cover under some low-hanging boughs on the lee side of the Divide. I got smug about my fat layer. I stayed warm, but Leland suffered from the cold. In some ways, women are better suited than men to long-distance hiking.

Summer dew glistens on a wildflower-enshrouded hillside on the road to Big Hole Pass.

CHIEF JOSEPH PASS TO LOWER SEYMOUR LAKE

—————▾▴▾—————

Anaconda-Pintler Wilderness, 79.1 miles

Chief Joseph Pass is 7,241 feet above sea level and far enough north to hold snow late into the hiking season. Thanks to easy access via a paved highway and relatively mellow terrain, it's a popular spot for cross-country skiing and snowmobiling. In the parking lot, a big sign announced "The Idaho/Montana Continental Divide National Scenic Trail was dedicated here on June 21, 1989. This segment extends north to Canada and south to Yellowstone National Park..." Yes, we knew that. When we were there, the lot was empty, the gravel shiny with rain, and despite the big sign, the continuation of the trail northward was not marked. It was all pretty dismal and put me in the mood to reflect on depressing stories from the past.

The Big Hole National Battlefield lies east of the pass. The largest of many skirmishes between the U.S. Army and the Nez Percé Indians took place there in 1877. Miscommunication and errors on both sides ended in tragedy for the tribe that had befriended Lewis and Clark. Chief Joseph led 500 women and children, and 300 Nez Percé warriors in a running battle that covered more miles than my brother and I hiked on the Continental Divide Trail. Near the Canadian border, the army caught up with the Nez Percé and Chief Joseph surrendered. He spent the next 26 years fighting for a better life for his people. "You might as well expect the rivers to run backward as that any man who was born free should be contented penned up and denied liberty to go where he pleases," Chief Joseph once said.

Colonel John Gibbon led the army forces at the Battle of the Big Hole, and Gibbons Pass, next stop on our trek, was named for him. The pass was a main route over the Divide, then more heavily traveled than it is today. In the lonely, muddy intersection of dirt tracks, I picked up a bullet casing that looked intriguingly antique. My father later identified it as a Winchester Special, a smokeless round designed to be reloadable with black powder, popular from 1895 to 1900. There is no way of knowing who fired the round or why, but its vintage places it squarely in the pioneering days of Montana's mining and logging industries.

The nearby Lost Trail Pass is one of many places where Lewis and Clark lost their way. They struggled through deep snows and were forced to eat some of their horses. That was about it for the stock of tragic tales I had to relate as Leland and I soldiered on toward Schultz Saddle. We met our support crew there, and we resupplied while they cleared deadfall from the trail.

Surveying a 360-degree view from the pass between Johnson Lake and Rainbow Lake in the Anaconda-Pintler Wilderness.

Opposite: Sunrise colors Upper Seymour Lake in the Anaconda-Pintler Wilderness.

Near the Anaconda-Pintler Wilderness border, we met a trio of Continental Divide hikers. One was a 78-year-old man—quite an inspiration to see someone that age still backpacking. He was discouraged to learn that he still had 17 miles to go before they came to a highway where they could hitchhike out for more supplies. A middle-aged man and woman made up the rest of the trio. They had hiked the Pacific Crest Trail in years past and said that it was much easier than the CDT.

From Schultz Saddle to Johnson Lake we breathed mosquitoes under a fish-belly sky. It rained on us and cleared up just in time for the clouds to mass again by afternoon and start the round of drizzles once more. Scenic views were few thanks to the thick trees. "On we went through this seeming endless forest of lodgepole pines. Sometimes they were tall, large and majestic, and for a way looked as though they had been planted in rows a certain distance apart by the hand of man. On we went over ridges, and across gulches in this eternal shade," observed Andrew Garcia in 1878. Garcia lived with a party of traders among the Indians in late 1800s Montana; his journals were later compiled in *Tough Trip Through Paradise*.

I got bored and started a mosquito kill-zone on my left forearm. I had twenty-eight mosquito carcasses on there before they started to dry and fall off.

Support crew quote:

"If we keep moving north at this rate, we can
stay in the mosquito season all summer long."

In spite of the rain, there was beauty to be seen and enjoyed. July is still spring in the high country, and the flowers were fresh and new In the rain they glowed like neon lights do in a city fog, the colors saturated and layered, infinitely deep.

South of Hope Lake, I was sitting in a meadow about 200 yards below the trail, filtering water from an unnamed tributary of Plimpton Creek when I heard a snorting, snuffing sound behind me. I turned to see a smallish black bear retreating through the brush. I yelled to hurry him on his way and to alert Leland, who was sheltering from the rain under some pines above me. Leland didn't get there in time to see the bear. I finished filtering water. It had been so quiet until the bear sniffed at me that his appearance and exit seemed to barely ripple the rainy, fogged-in silence.

The CDT passed above Hope Lake and we hiked off the trail about 100 yards to view the lake below us. A few glimpses of the Big Hole Valley also emerged through the trees. Although I told myself it was esoteric nonsense, I couldn't help but sense the ghosts of old catastrophes.

Seven more miles of hiking through mud and wet trees brought us to Elk Park, an alpine meadow above the Pintler Creek basin. Once again, the trail traversed below the ridge, missing the spectacular views to the north. We climbed a couple hundred feet and found not only Switzerland-like views of Pintler Peak and a ring of unnamed, rough companions, but also excellent camping with snowmelt for water, and dwarf conifers for protection from the wind. I washed with snow, a good "Leave No Trace" technique, and watched night flow into the valleys while the peaks

Lodgepole pines form a dense, multidimensional barrier north of Chief Joseph Pass on the Continental Divide.

Hope Lake, hidden here by low-lying clouds, is accessible from the CDT via a trail of steep switchbacks. This is one of the few lakes in the Anaconda-Pintler Wilderness that is closed to stock.

THE ANACONDA-PINTLER WILDERNESS

The Anaconda-Pintler Wilderness is named for the Anaconda Mountain Range and for Charles Pintler, a Big Hole Valley settler of the late 1800s. The 159,086-acre wilderness was designated in 1964. Special rules pertain to wilderness travel:

- *Party size is limited to 15 people.*
- *No motorized vehicles or equipment of any kind are allowed.*
- *Follow "Leave No Trace" backcountry guidelines.*
- *Observe camping restrictions near Johnson Lake.*
- *Additional regulations apply to stockmen.*
- *Wilderness permits are not required for backpackers, but registration at trailheads is requested.*

around us held the last, pale light. As always, we hung our food bags out of the reach of bears and far away from our tents. I snuggled into my sleeping bag and was halfway to sleep when another light rain came over the Divide, stealthy as a thief, sifting through the trees and into my dreams.

The descent to Pintler Creek was full of deadfall and bogs. My trekking pole was useful for log-walking and boulder-hopping. We saw about 50 elk on the climb up to Pintler Pass. The pass itself was only just clear of snow—we crossed a few snowfields getting down the north side. From the pass we could see Johnson Lake two miles below us, and a seemingly endless expanse of tree-covered ridges and creek drainages.

Though muddy when we were there, the trails in the Anaconda-Pintler Wilderness were well-signed and easy to follow with a few amusing exceptions. The CDT sign at Johnson Lake pointed straight out into the lake, as if hikers needed walking-on-water skills to continue. Johnson Lake was jumping with fish and showed signs of intensive camping. We left the CDT and hiked five miles out to a trailhead to meet our support crew. That five-mile stretch was heavily traveled by horses and mules. Don't step in the exhaust.

At the trailhead we saw a sign that proclaimed Pintler Pass was closed due to snow. "Whoops, that pass was closed, maybe we should turn around and go back." Our support crew was not at the trailhead. Uh-oh. There was no mention of the Continental Divide Trail on the signs, so maybe they were lost. We hiked another four or five miles down the road. We were losing the last of the daylight, so we hiked off the road a bit and set up camp. I ate trail mix in my tent and went to sleep. In the morning, Leland stayed with the gear while I hitchhiked down the road until I found our parents at one of the campgrounds. We dried

A sunset reflects in a seasonal pond in the Elk Park area of the Anaconda-Pintler Wilderness. Snow lingers in the passes here well into July, and snowmelt creates a multitude of small ponds and streams.

Located in the Anaconda-Pintler Wilderness, Warren Lake rests in a glacial cirque at 8,462 feet and seldom thaws before mid-June.

Near Upper Seymour Lake, a sign warns against leading stock onto this trail. The switchbacks, cut into a nearly vertical cliff by trail crews, are difficult, though not impossible, for stock to negotiate.

our gear in the sun and ate a second breakfast, then lunch, then a snack, then dinner, then a snack.

The next day, we hiked back to Johnson Lake and continued our trek, following the CDT east and northeast. The eastern half of the Anaconda-Pintler Wilderness was dryer and far more scenic—altogether a better hike. It was also arduous. The trail went down, up, down, up, down, up, down, around, and through. The tightly folded terrain presented us with one ridge after another, and each climb offered its own view of untamed land.

There were two "Rainbow" passes, one above Rainbow Lake and one near Rainbow Mountain. At the first Rainbow Pass, we met three more Continental Divide hikers. They were on their way to Mexico, but were keeping to a loose and easy agenda that included

The CDT passes through a forest of larches as it climbs to Goat Flat in the Anaconda-Pintler Wilderness. Here the trees cast a light, feathery shade where grasses and wildflowers grow.

hiking some portions of the trail north to south, and others south to north, with lots of hitchhiking in between. It was nice to meet a group whose priority was having a good time on the trail, and who were not too worried about finishing in one season. We discussed equipment with them, including buying the smallest backpack you can get by with for long-distance trekking, and then seeing who could pack the least amount of gear.

Rainbow Lake was a dark blue jewel, seen clearly at first from the switchbacking trail and then periodically through the trees. Miniature waterfalls and rivulets fed narrow bands of wildflowers in the rocks above the lake. Any approach to a lake on a forested trail is so aesthetically pleasing, when just a glimpse of water appears through the trees, and in the late evening there is a

Lynna Howard hikes the trail near Rainbow Mountain in the Anaconda-Pintler Wilderness. This part of the trail wends its way through groves of alpine larch.

moment when the lake holds the reflections of sun-blessed peaks and clouds. We camped at Warren Lake, though we had trouble finding a tent site clear of snow.

Near Cutaway Pass we came across a bear's fresh kill. A fawn had been bitten in half and the back half left on the trail. One of the most dangerous things a hiker can do is to pass a fresh kill, but we didn't see it until we were right on top of it. We lucked out in being able to pass by with no trouble. If you see a fresh kill the best bet is to give it as wide a berth as possible, and watch your back.

That was not the last of our adventures with wildlife. We camped in Queener Basin on July 25, and there were so many deer in the area that they ran into my tent during the night, knocking into tie-downs and pulling up stakes. I heard the drumbeat of hooves all around me, so I just covered my head with my arms and hoped for the best. Luckily, no harm was done.

The north sides of Cutaway Pass and Rainbow Pass #2 were decorated with extensive stands of alpine larches. These deciduous trees look

Switchbacks lead down from Goat Flat to Upper Seymour Lake in the Anaconda-Pintler Wilderness. Here steep terrain challenges the ingenuity of trail crews in this wilderness area west of Butte, Montana.

similar to an evergreen but the needles turn yellow-gold in the autumn. In spring and summer, the trees have a feathery profile that produces a gentle, dappled shade highly conducive to the growth of wildflowers and grasses. Below Rainbow Pass #2 we crossed a steep rock face and entered a stand of larches with a carpet of red Indian paintbrush and yellow buttercups. I hiked up and down the trail while Leland took photos.

On Goat Flat, where the trail began a descent to Upper Seymour Lake, a sign warned "Trail not recommended for stock." On the trail down to the lake we admired the stylings of the Anaconda-Pintler Wilderness trail crews: the best example we saw of expert rock work by a trail crew on a nearly vertical cliff.

Upper and Lower Seymour lakes are easily accessible from the east. We left the bears, elk, and deer behind to join a throng of day hikers, horsemen, and fishermen. After Labor Day, when the human visitors leave, Upper Seymour Lake has an entirely different aura. The eerie sound of elk bugling for their mates echoes off

Dawn's soft palette of golds and reds polishes the surface of Upper Seymour Lake in the Anaconda-Pintler Wilderness.

the surrounding cliffs, and ice edges the water. It's seven miles from Upper Seymour Lake to the improved campground and road at Lower Seymour Lake, a long way to hike in a heavy snowfall, so watch the weather if you visit in September.

Splitting the Anaconda-Pintler trek into two parts like we did is highly recommended. A strong hiker could probably do the first half from Chief Joseph Pass to Johnson Lake in about three days. The second half from the Middle Fork/Johnson Lake Trailhead to Lower Seymour Lake would take about four days. The Johnson Lake/Rainbow Pass/Rainbow Lake/Warren Lake/ Cutaway Pass/Queener Basin/Rainbow Pass #2/Page Lake/Goat Flat roller coaster required 7,372 feet of elevation gain (that's just gain, not loss).

Autumn turns the needles of larch trees to antique gold in the Anaconda-Pintler Wilderness.

Warren Lake is the highest lake on the route of the CDT through the Anaconda-Pintler Wilderness. Snowfields blanket its shores well into July.

LOWER SEYMOUR LAKE
TO ROGERS PASS

▼▲♥

Lower Seymour Lake to Champion Pass:
Fleecer, Highland, and Boulder mountains, 126.8 miles

The Fleecer, Highland, and Boulder mountains are lower, rolling hills compared to the glacier-carved peaks of the Anaconda-Pintler Wilderness. "Lower" is a relative term. We still had 8,400-foot ridges and peaks to cross, but most of the terrain was 6,000 to 7,000 feet in elevation. The hiking season on the Divide was so short that we pushed through this area in late May and early June, suffering mightily from the cold and wading through a lot of snow and mud.

The Continental Divide Trail swung southeasterly, climbing down off the top of the world to take a trip through a punishing underworld roofed with heavy clouds, storms, rain-darkened trees, and cold, white skies. The mountainsides ran with snowmelt. The air itself, the medium we breathed up and down the foggy slopes, was always full of some version of water—rain, hail, sleet, snow, mist, vapor, murk, and gloom. We hurried through the underworld just to shorten the misery. Along the way, I studied the finer points of cold, wet, and numb.

Rocky cliffs south of Rogers Pass catch an early snowfall in September.

Interesting cultural artifacts included the historic Mule Ranch on Highway 274, and the Hungry Hill Mine near Burnt Mountain. Like the Betty Ford Clinic, the Mule Ranch provided detox for four-legged beasts. Mules were used to pull ore carts in nearby mines and spent most of their lives underground breathing toxic fumes. Periodically, the mules rested and recovered at the ranch, now an incredibly picturesque tourist stop. Looking around at all the fine flora and fauna, it was hard to imagine that in the late 1880s the exhaust stack of the Anaconda Mine poisoned everything for miles around. There are still some active mines in the area. We took a wrong turn near the defunct Hungry Hill Mine and ended up at a mining company's "No Trespassing" sign.

It was hard to know where to hike and where not to hike in the Mount Haggin Wildlife Area. Unlike the rest of the trail, which is on federal land, this land is owned by the state and managed by Montana Fish and Wildlife, and trails were not signed. A locked gate east of the Mule Ranch made us wonder if we were on the right track. We were. We climbed over the gate and continued on the closed road.

Around the Hungry Hill Mine area there were some CD posts with the signs missing. Near the mine, derelict, ancient vehicles and rusting

Opposite: Early October brings a heavy snowfall to Stemple Pass. Cross-country ski trails connect Stemple, Flesher, and Rogers passes during the winter months.

Mules that worked in the Anaconda mines were taken to this "Mule Ranch" periodically for rest and rehabilitation. The historical site is now managed by Montana Fish and Wildlife.

mine machinery said as plain as words, "Dead dreams, played out." I swear that I could still smell the whiskey, mingling with the fog and rain.

We experienced most of the trail as a tunnel so I can't tell you much about the scenery. On a dim trail, walled by ghostly trees, we hiked up and we hiked down, knowing the open spaces more by the increase in winds than by sight. As T. S. Eliot said, "just the wrong time of year for such a journey." On the Divide, June is the cruelest month.

There was at times, however, an awkward and fitful beauty, spare moments of filtered sunlight catching the many-layered forest in dew-jeweled splendor. Then the light winked out as the clouds closed like a fist.

Everywhere we hiked near Butte and Helena, we found the skeletons of ancient cars. Some of the relics were so old that their shapes were reminiscent of buggies. These "buggies," rendered in metal, had been left to rust in the backwoods of

East of the Anaconda-Pintler Wilderness, the CDT crosses the Mount Haggin Wildlife Areas.

Montana. Sometimes no trace of a road lead to their graves. But, if we looked very closely, we could discern a faint remnant of a road, with five-to-eight-foot-tall pines colonizing its center. I deduced that the pioneers of the 1920s drove their cars like modern-day Montanans drive their all-terrain vehicles and pickup trucks.

Like a ghostly descendent of those early drivers, a white pickup truck appeared in our camp in the Highland Mountains. We were holed up inside the support crew's camper, waiting out a driving ice/rain/hail storm that howled around us, We were inside the cloud from which the spring storm issued. Almost drowned out by the thunder, a truck came shimmying and sliding up the road, roared sideways through our camp, slid 180 degrees around and, without stopping, slid out again, still driving sideways through the mud. The maneuvers were so extreme that we thought maybe the driver had been panicked by the intensity of

A late September ice and snow storm coats a weathered snag just south of Rogers Pass in the Helena National Forest.

A TERRITORY OF EXTREMES

Even where the Divide is lower, the terrain still pumps up the weather, creating extremes of wind, rain, and snow. There's a relentless aspect to the whole Divide—its length and imposing terrain; the exposure to the elements; the infinite views and equally endless forests; the cowboy loneliness of sections where humans have brought an entirely different culture and imprint to the trail; the long-abandoned line shacks and cabins through which the mountain winds blow unimpeded. Parts of the trail are so remote that "good access" equals any access you can find; other sections offer so much access that you get lost in a maze of roads. The Divide is a territory of extremes in every way.

A single heartleaf arnica flower finds a home in the notch of a multi-trunked conifer.

the storm and was looking for a way out. But later, when the cloud had lifted to just above our heads and the rain turned to a fine drizzle, we could hear the pickup in the distance, beating up some other road, pushing some other mud around.

You have guessed by now that much of this section is on roads and ATV trails. The Forest Service has plans for constructing new footpaths that bypass some of the roads, but the project had not even been flagged when we were there.

Lower Seymour Lake reflects the illusory warmth of clouds painted by the rising sun; the peaks of the Anaconda Range tower in the west.

Alpine forget-me-nots thrive near the peak of Red Mountain in the Highland Mountains.

In the drizzle, Leland and I got back on the trail. Near Delmoe Lake we met pack trains of four-wheelers heading into the hills. Some enterprising local lads had taken down every single Forest Service sign for miles in all directions, so we didn't know where the ATVs were heading and we certainly didn't know where we were supposed to go. In the nest of trails, many of them rutted into deep gullies, it was nearly impossible to find the one that led to the continuation of the CDT. We even found some motorcyclists who were as lost as we were. The riders seemed like regular folks, the

"There is nothing like the time when a rising sun and a sinking moon share the skyscape. It is worth stumbling out of your tent in the dark to climb some dim hill where you sit on a wet rock, shivering in the cold wind."

kind you would have seen on horses in the past, suited up to go hunting or fishing. There was, however, a fringe element of militaristic types: camo-fashioned, black-booted, skin-headed, dour-faced defenders of their version of the American Way.

Though they were only a few miles into the forest and the big city of Butte was a freeway-hop away, the military types carried extra gas cans (camo-painted, of course). A guy's gotta be ready, I guess. One group drove by us twice to look us over carefully, taking in

The CDT skirts the western edge of this wet meadow in Halfway Park, located in Deerlodge National Forest.

every detail to make sure that we were not the enemy. It was like walking into some gang's turf in the inner city. Worse yet, someone had even painted a few emblems of destruction on rock faces along the trail. This was no quick spray-paint job either, but house-high, clean-edged symbols (all black on the gray rocks) of things like lightning bolts, skulls married to swastikas, slogans, and a couple of phrases touting various forms of sexual perversion. The artists had added paeans to love as well: "Kevin + Mary = LOVE."

At one point, we heard round after round of ammunition being fired from a high-powered rifle, just over the ridge from where Leland was taking photographs. It was probably just target practice, but we could hear bullets ricocheting off rocks. Leland refused to be intimidated and kept on with his own shooting. I stood behind a rock for cover. Adding up the target practicing, the "rock art," and the intense scrutiny from the military types, we came to the conclusion that we should break the trail around Butte into long day hikes and not spend the night alone

"Rock art" is on display in Deerlodge National Forest near Homestake Pass.

in the Deerlodge National Forest. Our support crew was with us, so we met them at the end of each day.

This segment of the Continental Divide Trail will improve dramatically once the Forest Service has finished construction on trails that will stick closer to the Divide, cutting a much straighter path from Lime Kiln Springs to Pipestone Pass, and from Pipestone Pass to Homestake Pass. The foot trail north of Delmoe Lake to Interstate 15 was almost completed (though not signed) when we were hiking there.

We crossed Interstate 15 twice and Interstate 90 once. Between encounters with budding Rambos near the highways, the poetry of the trail was what we were accustomed to: the flow and change of wind, water, snow, rocks, and trees; a red-tailed hawk lolling about in the thermals above a meadow soaked by a flooding creek; wisps of gauzy clouds rising from spring grass and slowly ascending the mountainsides; and pungent pines with Stonehenge-like rocks in their shadowy depths.

By the way, we did finally find the Continental Divide Trail north of Delmoe Lake, but only after a full day of scouting by Leland. The Forest Service map did not show even half of the ATV trails, and it compounded our difficulties by showing the proposed CDT instead of the actual CDT. The rangers admitted that the people who put the CDT (complete with beautiful, easy-to-find symbols) on the map as it will be in about seven years were overly optimistic.

The topographic maps of the area showed even fewer roads than the Forest Service map. Almost the entire length of the trail around Butte winds its way through thick lodgepole pine forests, so it is not possible to navigate using landmarks on the topos. Occasionally, we crossed a recognizable watercourse, but even the creek crossings were not reliable because in the springtime everything is a watercourse.

We attacked the Delmoe Lake to I-15 section from the north also, finding switchback hell where Elk Creek Road ends and the trail begins.

The CDT passes many reminders of the pioneer dreams of the 1800s. Here, the remains of a log cabin are nearly covered by tall grasses in the moist swale along the Boulder River.

There were so many switchbacks up the mountainside that the whole thing was like a terraced garden. In places, the trail would go for 500 feet along the side of the mountain before the next switchback, and the grade was so shallow that it could have been a wheelchair ramp (except for the rocks and stumps). Those switchbacks added about three miles to the trail, but I guess they've solved the erosion problem. Above the switchbacks, we came to more unsigned trail intersections.

Ranger quote, in reply to the question, "Where is the trail?": "Let me know when you find it."

There was more road-walking where the trail crossed I-15 near Sheepshead Mountain Recreation Area. We were happy because we had finished circling Butte. We made our way to Lowland Campground and, at last, turned north again. Olson Road climbs through a lodgepole forest; occasional clearings created by previous logging efforts provided limited views of the Elkhorn Mountains to the east/ northeast.

The road became a trode (a trail/ road hybrid), rutted and steep, hemmed in by trees. Once again, beware the perfidy of maps that show the CDT marching along the Divide. That's a proposed route, virtual, not real. We hiked about 10 miles out of our way before we figured out the correct path.

In the evening we camped below a nameless knoll, and the skies miraculously cleared. Leland and I climbed to a high spot to look the situation over. Fog and low-lying clouds still stole through the valleys, with every stream and river marked not by the sparkle of water, but by a wavy blanket of mist.

The next morning, at the awful hour of 4:30 a.m., we climbed to the top of the knoll again and were rewarded once more with ethereal scenes out of some master watercolorist's book of idealized mountain settings. This time, the near-full moon also hung over the snowy spires of the Bitterroots to the west. There is nothing like the time when a rising sun and a sinking moon share the skyscape. It is worth stumbling out of your tent in the dark to climb some dim hill where you sit on a wet rock, shivering in the cold wind.

At Champion Pass (signed as "Champion Pass"—whoopee!) the CDT crosses the dirt road and continues north. At the pass there was a

An up-close view of autumn colors is found in the lodgepole pine forest between Flesher Pass and Rogers Pass.

post that used to have CD signs on it, but the signs were gone when we were there. Someone had written "CD" on the post itself with a marking pen, a helpful message that held up remarkably well in the rain.

Champion Pass to Rogers Pass: Boulder Mountains and Lewis and Clark Range, 111.2 miles

A lot of people have asked how my brother and I managed to hike the Continental Divide Trail and still have a life. We stayed on the trail for two or three weeks out of every month during the hiking season, then we rushed home to rescue the rest of our lives. As a result, we did a lot of driving and so did our support crew. We got very familiar with all the approach routes on both sides of the Divide, and I can now ready my backpack in about 15 minutes. Need breeds speed.

We lost count of how many times we had to drive through Butte, Montana. The farther north we progressed on the trail, the longer the drives got. From an early morning start, we arrived at Champion Pass late in the afternoon. We ate a hasty meal in light rain, then packed up and headed out. I was almost in a panic to hurry onward. I definitely did not want to get stopped by snow again, and wanted even

The sun sets over Bald Butte in the Helena National Forest.

less to have to come back and do this section of trail later. We pushed on, with very little of the topography visible around us. It rained every time we lost elevation and snowed whenever we climbed.

Ranger quote: "June is the rainy season in Montana ...when it's not snowing."

Responses from other clever Montana wits in answer to the question, "How do you know it's springtime in Montana?":

When it's warm enough by noon to take off your long underwear.

When the settlers in the valley start shootin' off fireworks.

When the snowmelt carries off the whiskey bottles you threw out the front door.

When it doesn't snow for a whole week at a time.

When the forest rangers leave the office.

The elegantly rusting hulk of a 1930s vintage automobile sits in the weeds in Marysville.

We had both Forest Service maps and topographic maps with us, but still had to hunt for the route of the CDT. When we hiked the trail, it was erratically and inadequately signed on the ground, but has since been improved.

North of Blizzard Hill, there were two CDT signs—a sign noting the mileage to Leadville (incorrectly), and a trail register. We found our way to the ghost town of Leadville, but it was hard to tell where to go next.

Let me tell you about Leadville. It was mid-June by the time we got there, and Leadville was still seriously snowed in. There *was* almost enough melt-water to carry away the whiskey bottles. There were several abandoned cabins, all fallen into ruins, and some old machinery that bred sympathy for the mules that had to haul it up there. Due to the lay of the land, the sun seldom shines in Leadville. Even July 4th might be too early for spring. At an elevation of 7,880 feet, Leadville is trapped in a basin of trees, beat upon by storms

PAST MEETS PRESENT

Prehistoric forces laid the foundations for the gold and silver rush that spawned the boomtown of Marysville, Montana, in 1876. The usual fossils and ancient evidence of volcanic activity are proof for the inevitable "Millions of years ago..." explanation that puts Montana under water, sea creatures swimming where her mountain ranges now stand, volcanoes doing their part to ensure the percolation of gold, silver, lead, zinc, copper, coal, and sapphires to the surface.

Today, the most evident "fossils" are the dilapidated buildings, cars, cabins, and mine shafts that litter the landscape. The past is mixed with the present. Old buildings lean against new. The town has not been gussied up for the tourist trade, but it does have a post office that accepts general delivery packages for hikers.

In the former mining town of Marysville, Montana, the ghosts of the past live side by side with present-day businesses.

that come early and stay late. In places, we were slogging through two feet of snow while rain poured down on our heads. When we stopped hiking, we got cold. We refined our definitions of miserable.

Thanks to the snow, we missed the trail to Cottonwood Lake. Rather than give up, we struggled onward through downed timber, trying to follow the new route. No one can say we didn't try, but in the end we had to backtrack to Champion Pass and follow the dirt road for about nine miles eastward to intercept a marked trail to Thunderbolt Mountain. In part, it was a matter of safety. We were singing the Leadville Hypothermic Blues and had to give up before we lost what little judgment we had. Hypothermia is particularly insidious because it reduces your ability to reason.

The trailhead south of Thunderbolt Mountain told us that the Continental Divide Trail was ahead, plus it pointed the way to Cottonwood Lake. Much better. And besides, the road was open in June and looked like a different country altogether than did the netherworld around Leadville.

Our support crew was stunned when we returned from this latest battle. I was so wet that moisture had made its way through my raingear and all the layers beneath. I was glad to partake of hot food at the Mobile Wilderness Cafe.

I assumed, wrongly, that my activity level, coupled with the cold weather, would preclude any possibility of weight gain. I ate pecan pie, among other things, all of them tasty. I continued this routine for the remainder of the trip. When I got home I found that I had gained two pounds. Leland had lost weight. I gained weight! Incredible. I ought to

be the subject of scientific experiments. Oh well, muscles under a layer of fat is a bear's survival mode. Maybe it would work for me.

Ever northward we wended our way, eventually finding MacDonald Pass in a cap of clouds. Leland's photo opportunities were limited. One day he only took two photographs, one of an impressive pile of horse manure sprouting a bouquet of mushrooms (you had to be there), and one of a delicate array of corn lilies imbued with subdued light and gleaming with raindrops. So, he took photos of poisonous plants and piles of poop. I reported this photographic success to the support crew and it made them proud to be a part of the team.

South of MacDonald Pass, we saw a big black bear. This bear sighting made an even dozen on the Continental Divide for me, five grizzlies and seven black bears. Our MacDonald Pass bear sped up an extremely steep hill and over boulders the size of cars as if he were on a racetrack. It was an awesome display of power. Concrete evidence that you can't outrun a bear.

I hiked the few miles between Priest Pass and Mullen Pass by myself. It turned out to be more exciting than I had anticipated. The trail was very hard to find in some areas, and private land holdings that were newly fenced forced me farther and farther east. The trail appeared and disappeared periodically. There was one particularly bad spot where the trail crossed an old railroad grade. The correct trail looked like a game trail, while a well-established path marked with a blazed tree angled west. I walked half-a-mile down the wrong trail before I figured out my mistake and backtracked. The game trail eventually improved into cut tread, but not before I had come across lots of black bear scat. That woke me up.

The moon lingers on the horizon as the rising sun lights the snowcapped Bitterroot Range.

A lone tree stands sentinel over Meyers Hill near Dana Spring in the Helena National Forest.

I was keeping a sharp lookout when I spotted what looked like a large dog running through rocks and trees above me. I thought that Leland was probably out looking for me because I was overdue and had sent his dog, Tempest, on ahead to sniff me out. I called, "Hey, Tempest. Hey, girl!" But the "dog" was very startled. It jumped, whirled to look in my direction, growled once, and then sped away at top speed. My guess: I was downwind of a wolf and it didn't see me until I had shouted. "Well," I said out loud, "I thought wolves were supposed to be social creatures." I would have been happier to see Tempest. I eventually made my way to where Leland was waiting to pick me up.

I think that if one more person tells me that the Continental Divide Trail should not be signed and that it should be difficult to find in order to provide hikers with "the thrill of discovery" or "with a true wilderness experience," I'm going to pop them one. After hiking hundreds of miles, I was tired of misleading signs and blazes, tired of unsigned routes, and tired of backtracking to find the trail. I like exploring and even getting a little lost on short backpacking trips, but long-distance jaunts are different. There is not enough extra food, energy, and time; not enough margin of safety in long-distance trekking. Besides, I have experienced the "thrill of discovery" big time and many times. Mother Nature provides plenty of thrills along the Continental Divide. Also, in the Montana/Idaho section, no one needs to worry about gentrification of the trail at this point. Land managers need to focus on making it feasible to find the trail most of the time.

While I am indulging in this diatribe about signs, who designed the wooden Continental Divide Trail signs anyway? They consist of a vertical arrow between a "C" and a "D." This means that there is an apparently directional arrow on every CD sign, but it always points straight ahead (or to Heaven). Additional directional arrows are often absent and/or weathered away. My advice is to take each CD sign as proof that you are currently standing on the correct route, but don't assume any more than that, and look over any arrows with narrow-eyed suspicion.

Hikers should also learn to recognize a CD post that is signless. The posts are of a uniform size and the rectangle where the sign is missing is a sure sign. Continental Divide Trail signing, where it exists, is a disaster and will have to be completely replaced.

In an open meadow north of Mullen Pass, we confronted several four-wheel-drive tracks and one CDT sign on a tree. Pop quiz:

1. Are any of the visible tracks the correct CDT route?
Answer: No.

2. Can you see the next CDT sign or post from the tree?
Answer: No.

3. Where is the next CDT sign?
Answer: On an upslope tree, under drooping branches where it is well-protected from the weather and from view.

In spite of the sadistic signs, we kept going north. Marysville, an old mining town northwest of Helena, is only three miles off the Continental Divide Trail. That's close, by our standards, so we stopped to investigate.

Grasses south of Rogers Pass bow their heads beneath a coat of heavy September frost.

Signs warned fishermen about eating fish from the streams, which are laced with mercury or other toxic chemicals. That gave me pause. What about the water we had been filtering from streams? Maybe I would go back to melting snow.

On Black Mountain, northwest of the Marysville area, the CDT route was marked two different ways. One route was a dead end on top of the mountain. The correct route contoured around the east side of the mountain. I felt the thrill of discovery.

Even on well-signed parts of the trail, I had some nifty wilderness experiences, including more encounters with the weather gods. Near Rogers Pass, gusty winds brought saturated clouds out of the valleys and up onto the Divide, where they proceeded to flatten the glacier lilies with three inches of hail. I hunkered in the lee of a tree while thunder and hailstones beat around me. I was well-dressed in clothes and fat, so I took a nap. When I woke up, my hiking boots were buried in hail. It looked so pretty that it made me quite happy.

It occurs to me that I have been transformed by this expedition. I nap through hailstorms, I wash in snowbanks (so much better than polluting a stream, and the granules make a fine scrubbing compound), I think clothes that are merely damp are dry, and I hesitate to tell you what my standards are for "clean." I have been transformed—but into what, I'm not sure.

Between Stemple Pass in the south and Rogers Pass in the north, the CDT wends its way through seemingly endless lodgepole pine forests. Grasses, sedges, ferns, and broadleaf herbs form a delicate understory in the shade of the trees.

ROGERS PASS
TO MARIAS PASS

Rogers Pass to Benchmark:
Scapegoat Wilderness in the Lewis and Clark Range, 65.3 miles

At the start of our journey, near Rogers Pass, northwest of Helena and south of the Scapegoat Wilderness, we met three rangers from the Lincoln District of the Helena National Forest. These three, clean, pressed and pleated guys were there to inspect recent work on the Continental Divide National Scenic Trail. They gave us the scoop on new routes, misinformed us about the lack of water, and told us grizzly stories.

Here's the best of their grizzly stories. A woman was backpacking through the area to study the grizzly habitat and was very intent on following all the rules for avoiding harmful encounters with the bears. She was hanging her food in a tree per the rules, using the "rock-in-a-sock" method: one puts a rock in a sock, ties a rope to the sock, throws same over a high branch, and then uses the rope to haul the food up. Only this time, the rock gained momentum, swung like a pendulum, and came back to thwack the woman on the forehead. Blood everywhere. The rangers had to rescue her.

Modern-day cowboys Gregg Funk and Herman Brune take a coffee break in the Bob Marshall Wilderness.

The Rangers also had tales to tell of a grizzly "getting rambunctious" on some rancher's land. They warned us not to camp in the first 9.5 miles (from Rogers Pass to Red Mountain) where camping is prohibited because of the grizzlies. New ruling. Well, sheesh, we didn't know and it was already noon. Too late in the day for us to hike 9.5 miles of up-and-down terrain with our backpacks on.

We looked at the map and quickly figured the miles. Okay, we could make Alice Creek, about seven miles, and we could camp off the Divide. We locked the truck, hefted our packs and were off. A hot day. Maybe the only hot day of the Montana summer. Sweat rolled off my forehead into my eyes, the miles slowly rolled away behind us. We looked back from a high point and saw the snake-like contours of the Divide. Tree-covered mountains, a few rocky interludes, bare saddles, no other humans, the usual. Then we spotted the water. Okay, this had to be Alice Creek, the only water for miles the rangers had said. Sure seemed like a quick seven miles. We camped.

The creek ran prettily between wildflowers and a few pines; and it was easily accessible water, with decent camping a few hundred yards below the Divide. We figured we were off the Divide and therefore out of the no-camping zone, though what 300 yards means

Opposite: Ahorn Creek near Indian Point Meadows in the Bob Marshall Wilderness. This creek flows north to meet the Sun River.

Arrowleaf balsamroot grows on the east side of the Front Range of the Rocky Mountains.

to a grizzly I don't know. We were also, though we didn't know it at the time, lost. We thought we were at Alice Creek because the rangers had been so specific about the water. We almost got more lost the next morning, trying to make the topography around us match the Alice Creek area. We finally figured out our mistake, that we were on Bear Creek. We noted that the entire ridge above our camp had been rototilled by bears, every rock overturned. Now we had no doubt that we were in the Grizzly Corridor.

From Alice Creek going north on the Divide, we tried to follow a few elk-nibbled and faded ribbons the rangers had hung in the trees the year before to mark new trail construction. We lost the "trail" several times and had to scout for more ribbons. Once we sat down and ate wild strawberries for a while, cursing the rangers. We looked uphill from our strawberry patch to see another ribbon where, with indecipherable ranger wisdom, the trail turned to send us back parallel to the way we had come. Future switchbacks probably, erosion control, something like that.

As Leland and I neared the border of the Scapegoat Wilderness, we came across more and more areas that had burned in 1988. More acreage burned in the Scapegoat and Bob Marshall Wilderness Areas than in Yellowstone, but Yellowstone got all the media coverage. As we walked along, we could see where the fire hadn't been stopped by normal breaks, like ridges bare of fuel. It just went on and on.

I had a dreamlike, effortless feeling as we hurried along a high, open ridge just south of the wilderness border. We were trying to outpace a thunderstorm. As we cruised along at top hiking speed, it was if my steps, the pushing off from the earth to send my body forward, kept the earth-ball rolling. As the ball rolled under me, the storm-filled horizon came nearer and nearer, until we had to abandon the ridge and scurry into the protection of a small grove of trees that had not burned. Backpacking is usually terribly hard work for me. I must have finally gotten into good enough shape to enjoy a few moments of almost effortless hiking.

The storm blew by, missing us by about half-a-mile. We climbed back up to the crest of the Divide and hiked on. The standing dead of all those burned trees looked, from a distance, like some kind of strange growth, a wiry crew cut of fur or hair. It was mouse-gray with a carpet of wildflowers and green saplings emerging beneath.

Bighorn Lake, an azure jewel surrounded by cliffs, lay 1,000 feet below the trail—too steep and too long a climb for water unless one was desperate. Subalpine fir, Engelmann spruce, and whitebark pine used to grow here. Now their weathered trunks had a silvery sheen in the afternoon light. The uninterrupted wind blasted through the burned trees without the usual susurration, the whisper and rustle that is the wind's voice in a live forest.

The wind, as we followed the Divide in that first week of August, grew cold and smelled like snow. It caught my backpack

Fall color touches low-lying shrubs and grasses near timberline on the south face of Crown Mountain.

A waterfall in the Bighorn Creek area offers respite from the miles of burned forest in the Scapegoat Wilderness.
Previous page: Bean Lake mirrors sunset clouds on the road to the Dearborn River Trailhead
near the border of the Scapegoat Wilderness.

on the switchbacked turns and tried to push me off the mountain. The day before had been so hot that I cut the sleeves off of my hiking shirt. That must have made the weather gods laugh. A cold front swept down on us with a vengeance, later keeping its snow promise and adding golf-ball-sized hail for good measure.

I had to dig deep to find the will to stand up to the wind, performing a rough ballet of jockeying and shuffling for balance. Plant a trekking pole, then step—plant and step, plant and step. A female thought, "No doubt I'm ruining my complexion here, paying in skin for fighting with the wind."

The big burn of 1988 also affected watercourses. Year-round streams that appeared on the topographic maps no longer ran. The upper reaches of Bighorn Creek were dry. Two creeks flanking a pond where the trail skirts Caribou Peak were dry, leaving us with only the diminished pond as a watersource.

It was at the pond that the golf-ball-sized hail caught up with us. Leland put Tempest inside his tent so the dog wouldn't get knocked out. I decided that if I was going to die, I would at least be well-fed, so I sat in my tent as the hail pummeled it and I ate nut butter on bagel crisps, watching the balls of hail mound up as they rolled off the tent fly.

We couldn't have camped in a colder, danker spot. The cirque that housed the pond was steep and deep, like being in a fish bowl. The trees showed signs of being matted down by snow up to about 20 feet. Black and dark brown moss hung from black

Fireweed and other opportunistic plants bloom profusely beneath the blackened trunks left by the 1988 Scapegoat Wilderness fires.

Bright red rosehips announce the arrival of autumn on the banks of the Dearborn River in the Scapegoat Wilderness.

branches. Far above us, a departing cumulus cloud caught the sun we couldn't see and briefly cast a pink reflection into the midge-filled pond. A tawny deer, the color of ripe wheat, passed through the dark forest not 10 feet away from my tent. The bright, warm color of the deer looked like a light in all that shadow.

In that light-forsaken and desolate spot so far from everywhere, there were still signs of human trespass. Some idiot (or idiots) had left a broken whiskey bottle and some empty cans in a fire ring. Who would bother to carry whiskey all that way? But because they had, this was definitely the place to drink it.

The next morning we climbed out of the hole, glad to have found some sun. Here in the seldom-used reaches of the Scapegoat Wilderness, some of the trails were not constructed to the usual standards. Switchbacks were nonexistent or very steep. Trail tread appeared and disappeared. Trails in designated wilderness areas are usually better. Sometimes we hiked for as long as 10 miles without seeing a sign. "Where the hell are we?" was a frequent question. Our topos and overall maps showed green trees where there were none, water where it was dry, wilderness boundaries that did not match the locations on the ground.

The Bighorn Creek Trail was called "Sheep Creek" on the ground. Discrepancies like that can be so confusing. Apparently, the locals call it Sheep Creek, excuse me, make that "crick." There are no creeks in Montana, only cricks. Never met a forest ranger or native Montanan yet that called a stream of water a "creek." Leland says they've spelled it wrong on all the signs.

There are only so many miles of burned forest one can walk through before appreciation begins to fade for the young, eternal spring-green of saplings, the purple heads of fireweed, and the clumps of paintbrush. From the top of every pass, the vista of burned trees was disheartening. Grouse seemed to like it, though. Flocks of them wandered through the ghostly trees or just sat on the trail, living up to their nickname of "Fool Hens."

We were pleased to come down into Landers Fork, which had escaped the fire, and was very delightfully laid out with intersecting streams, open meadows, and flat camping spots. Leland set up his tent next to a tree that bore the claw marks of a BIG bear. The marks were old, though, and there are bears everywhere, so we stayed. That night I thought I heard someone or something brushing against my tent. "Go away!" I shouted, but the soft brushing continued. I looked out. It was snowing.

By morning we were inundated by a full-scale snowstorm with a driving wind behind it. I huddled over my oatmeal to keep it from filling up with snow. I took my tent down in record time and packed it up wet. We had to start walking in order to stay warm. Remember, this was still in the first half of August. The good news: no mosquitoes.

The Scapegoat and Bob Marshall Wilderness Areas are so deep and wide that the mountains can make their own weather. It can be a warm, dry summer on the edges where sensible folks live, but snowing like hell in the middle. It was still snowing, but very lightly, when we reached the pass above the Dearborn River Valley. What looked liked a straightforward descent on our maps looked like a four-way intersection on the

Indian paintbrush flowers under the North Wall in the Bob Marshall Wilderness.

ground. Snow, wind, and fog partially obscured the pass. We looked at our maps, we looked at the unsigned intersection, we cursed. We opted for the trail with the most horse manure, figuring it had to lead to the Dearborn River Trailhead. Good guess.

The lower reaches of the Dearborn also escaped the fire. For hikers who just want to do a short jaunt on the Continental Divide Trail, the Dearborn serves as a good access point. At the lower elevations, stands of aspen and cottonwood trees mix with the pines, and the river is clear and pretty (but be prepared to ford it a few times). Slight elevation changes occur where the trail parallels the river. It is a milder, mellower version of the Continental Divide Trail. Even the drive to the trailhead is a winner, with excellent views of the massive Front Range of the Rockies. The Divide hides behind the Front Range, a wall behind a wall.

We had enough food with us for the long hike from Rogers Pass to Benchmark, but like all backpackers, we were always hungry anyway. There comes a time when the syrupy light of late afternoon, lying like sweetened butter on a buttress of rocks decked with lichen and moss feeds the spirit, but not the body. Leland conjectured that if we broke into one of the locked guard stations, there would be pancake and waffle mix in there. Syrup even. Painfully, we hiked on by.

The Scapegoat and Bob Marshall Wilderness Areas are cheek-to-cheek. Together with the Great Bear Wilderness and Glacier National Park, they make up one long grizzly bear corridor. The southern half of the Scapegoat is virtually unused by humans. We met our first and only fellow hikers on this trip near Welcome Pass, at about 45 miles into our hike. As we neared the Bob Marshall Wilderness border and the Benchmark access point, we saw signs of horsemen using the trail, but we were still all alone.

After hiking 65 miles in almost total isolation, we came out with a jolt at Benchmark. Benchmark has not one, not two, but four parking lots for horse trailers. There are overflow parking lots, commercial outfitter parking lots, an airstrip, and, oh yes, one small parking lot for hikers.

At Benchmark we met our outfitters, two cowboys and one cowgirl whom we had hired to help us through the next 100 miles. Yes, boys and girls, you may think we wimped out in requiring some help, and you are free to make disparaging comments when you have hiked more than 600 miles, carrying your home on your back.

Indian paintbrush thrives in the Caribou Peak area, where the forest canopy was reduced by the Scapegoat Wilderness fires.

Benchmark to Marias Pass:
The Bob Marshall Wilderness, Lewis and Clark Range, 122.6 miles

Between Benchmark in the south and Marias Pass in the north, there are no good access points to the Continental Divide Trail. 10- to 12-mile hikes over steep passes separate the Divide from access roads, and those seldom-traveled roads are at least 40 miles from the nearest town. This section of trail was the longest and most inaccessible trek we faced, and that was the least of our troubles.

In the Bob Marshall Wilderness, hell wasn't fire and brimstone, it was mud. Mudholes, bogs, seeps, swamps, fens, marshes. You name it, if it was wet, "The Bob" had it. Mudholes so deep that pack mules got mired in them. The horses and mules didn't make the bogs, they just made them worse. When we were hiking instead of riding, we got muddy up to our knees. Supposedly, there have been dry years—after all, much of it burned in 1988—but it was wet when we were there, and the local outfitters told me that there were usually some bogs to negotiate, even in dry years.

My notes from Open Creek and Fool Creek read: "Air as damp and cold as a druid's breath. Grizzly tracks in the mud. Frequent bog holes that suck at the legs of horses, mules, and hikers with democratic indifference. Trees festooned with dark moss that looks like dead hair, or eerie veils where only infrequent sun penetrates."

The critical factor was time. There were places where the mud would slow a hiker to one mile per hour, the same toll that very steep terrain normally takes. Riding horses through part of this section solved the problem. Hikers planning a twelve- to fourteen-day trip, can also arrange for an outfitter to bring in resupplies at the halfway point.

The number and quality of interesting side trips also factored in to our decision to hire some help. Prairie Reef Lookout, Beartop Lookout, Moonlight Peak, Biggs Creek Flat, and others are all well worth visiting.

A mule packer leads his string below the "Chinese Wall" in the Bob Marshall Wilderness.

If you've already taken the trouble to slog through the mud on the access trails, you might as well make the extra effort to see the good stuff.

The two cowboys who worked on our expedition were from Oklahoma and Texas; the cowgirl, Annie, was a local. Apparently, most of the local Montana cowboys preferred cows to people. Also, mule packing, as I was to learn, is a complicated affair requiring a lot of skill, experience, and muscle.

Gregg, from Oklahoma, told this story: "If a mule bites you, you bite him back. I had a mule bite me on the shoulder once. I pulled his upper lip back so I could see that nice, pink tender stuff and chomped down on him hard. He hasn't even tried to bite anybody since." It was no tall tale. He had witnesses. Here's another quote from Gregg regarding getting into the saddle on cold mornings: "That saddle can be so cold it'll suck yer eyeballs in."

Herman, a championship saddle bronc rider (with buckle to prove it), "student of female behavior," and wannabe writer from Texas, told this story: "I had some hunters with me and was leading a string of mules off of a Tennessee Walker. That Tennessee Walker could walk some. He walked fast enough to jerk the heads off of them mules. So when I seen that sassy-assed coyote that had been after Jimmy's dog, I didn't want to pass up the opportunity. I gave my mules to the other handler and took out after that coyote, building me a loop on the way. You think I could get that Tennessee Walker up to speed? Hell no. He couldn't run fast enough to scatter his own shit. That coyote looked back at me, grinnin', and I chased him all over hell and back again looking for a chance to throw down and never got one. Entertained the hunters, though."

From Benchmark, near the southern end of The Bob, to Beaver Lake at the northern border, Leland and I traveled in the company of A Lazy H Outfitters. We walked some and rode some, with Leland walking about half the time to protect the camera equipment he carried. I walked to explore the side trips we wanted to list in the guidebook and walked to relieve sore muscles.

In the Sun River Game Preserve we saw a grizzly, a blond yearling that paralleled our track for a while and then hung around to watch the mule train pass by. On the West Fork of the South Fork of the Sun River (don't get me started on these names) we saw one huge bear print, plain as a carving in the mud of the trail. In several other creek drainages we saw sow and cub prints. Deer in the preserve were fearless and walked through camp at a leisurely enough pace to stop for munchies here and there. It was like a big, open zoo—but a dangerous one. Hikers have to take every precaution to store their food properly and to avoid encounters with the residents.

The most famous geological formation in The Bob is the "Chinese Wall," a 1,000-foot-high escarpment that marks the Continental Divide in such an unmistakable way that no other division of the Pacific and Atlantic drainage

An outfitter's portable kitchen is a welcome sight for a hungry long-distance trekker.

THE WILD, WILD BOB

An unexpected side effect of the designation of large wilderness areas is the preservation of America's "Wild West" skills and ways. No roads and no mechanized equipment of any kind are allowed in the wilderness. Two-man crosscut saws, bucksaws, mule packers, horse wranglers, guns, knives of all kinds, and men who are tough as nails and twice as hard come with the territory. This is especially true in a Wilderness Area like "The Bob," where the area's sheer size makes traversing it on foot a daunting prospect. The Bob, the Great Bear, and Scapegoat add up to more than 1.5 million acres of wilderness—that's 2,400 square miles (6,215 square kilometers) that is known collectively as Bob Marshall Country.

systems is clearer along the entire route from Mexico to Canada. The 12-mile-long wall looks like the arrested motion of a breaking wave. In some ways, this is an accurate representation. It's just that the wave is in super-slow motion.

About 175 million years ago, the tectonic plate bearing the North American continent collided with the floor of the Pacific Ocean and broke along the margin. The floor of the ocean began to slide into the resultant trench and down into the mantle, a very hot place that melts rock and sometimes sends it spewing back up to the surface. The plate collision set the stage for the Rocky Mountains to come. Thick slices of the upper crust got pushed together like a loosely folded map. About 70 million years ago, some of the folds broke along fault lines and were pushed farther eastward—hence the long, chopped-off, and stacked-up slabs of older rock that come to an abrupt end where Montana's high plains begin. That's a short version of a long and complicated geological story, but it accounts for the overthrust block of the Front Range, and for the Chinese Wall.

Ruffed grouse can be seen often along the CDT. The "Fool Hens" think they are hidden if they do not move.

Wind from the west pushed cloud masses over the Wall, where they broke up like ships hitting a reef. Just under the tattered clouds, on narrow shelves decorated with rims of grass and pine trees, we saw mountain goats grazing. The Wall was neither as high nor as colorful as some of the canyon walls in southern Utah, but it was impressive, perhaps more so because it came as such a relief from the claustrophobic approach routes up the narrow creek drainages.

The Wall really consists of two parts, the Chinese Wall and the North Wall. We saw lots of people, including nine hikers and multitudes of riders, at the Chinese Wall and none at the North Wall. Only outfitters, occasional trail crews, and crazed CDT hikers venture along the arduous North Wall route. Highlights of the North Wall route included Sock Lake and Lake Levale. Sock Lake, hidden from view, hung in a high cirque accessible only by a steep scramble. Lake Levale was just off the trail and colored with glacial silt to a matte-finish aqua reminiscent of 1950s kitchen decor.

Gregg and Herman, who looked like they were almost asleep in the saddle most of the time, went through a change resembling alchemy when they wrangled the horses and mules. They drove the stock through a riffle of white water on Trail Creek at dawn one morning. The animals weren't used to that route and tried to diverge, but the cowboys expertly herded them across it at a run. Slivers of the stream leapt up from their hooves into the morning light. I couldn't see the decisions being made, just that the cowboys and the horses were always where they needed to be at every moment, wheeling and running, completely one entity.

With no self-consciousness whatsoever, both cowboys wore leather chaps, beat-up hats, bandannas, the whole rigmarole—all of it worn to a fine patina in places and black with dirt in others. Gregg did show some pride in his boots, tucking his jeans in so the red tops would "shine like a beacon."

As "cookie girl," I was responsible for shaking an enticing pan of horse treats in front of the temporary rope corral when the stock was brought in just before dark and again in the morning. My job was to face the running herd of mules and horses as the cowboys and Annie drove them toward the corral. I stood my ground until the last minute and then ducked into the corral and under the rope at the far side with several thousand pounds of mules and horses hot on my heels. This usually went as planned and was more scenic than dangerous, but one evening Annie was in front of the herd twirling her wrangling reins to keep the stock behind her as Gregg and Herman pushed from behind. Annie's horse acquired a bee on its rump and began to dance sideways. She tried for control, but it was impossible and the horse spun circles at the corral entrance, knocking me to one side but not hurting me. I jumped away as I was being hit, so it wasn't bad— didn't even spill my "cookies."

Another one of my jobs was holding each mule by a lead rope as the cowboys threw the packs up onto them and lashed the

A footpath winds through lodgepole pines near the Two Medicine River in Glacier National Park.

The West Fork of the South Fork of the Sun River, Bob Marshall Wilderness.

loads tight. Most of the mules just stood there patiently, but a couple of the younger ones would try to dance around. I learned to imitate Herman, cocking my head, and saying in a Texas drawl with some menace behind it, "Be sweet. (Bay suhweet)" That worked most of the time. When "Be sweet" didn't work, Herman told me to "talk mean to them." So I let go with "Rastus, you dumb sonuvabitch, come here!" The cowboys doubled over laughing. Rastus stepped up nicely. Herman said, "Well, I guess he's heard that one before."

We faced one big disaster on this trip—Leland got lost. On what was to be the last leg of our journey with the outfitters, Leland decided to leave camp early and walk a bit on his own. This was not unusual for him, as he often went off alone to take photos. Still, I felt an unmistakable premonition of trouble as I watched him leave with his camera gear and the dog. I should have acted on that premonition.

I packed Leland's lunch and rain jacket on his horse. We were at least an hour behind Leland and didn't expect to see him for a while. I half-heartedly looked for his and Tempest's tracks, but I knew he'd be stepping off the trail to go around the mud. Annie's mother, Sally, had joined the expedition by then. She was an excellent tracker and the first to distinguish dog tracks from the numerous coyote tracks. We all felt somewhat relieved.

Bad news showed up in the form of two hikers with a German shepherd like Tempest. We asked them to keep an eye out for Leland and

"The horses were running in a cloud on invisible hooves, their manes and tails a darker silver in the gray fog. The bell mare's bell sounded sad and bright at the same time. Where was my brother?"

to tell him to stop and wait for us if they saw him before we did. I was getting more worried. Leland without his lunch, Leland skipping lunch, was the worrisome detail. He's so thin that he doesn't have any fat reserves to hike on. He doesn't skip meals.

The trail up to Badger Pass was sprinkled with open meadows called "parks," and nice views of Cap Mountain and Whiskey Ridge through scattered trees. Strawberry Creek was clear as glass and running enough water to be called a river. It would have been a good day if I'd known where Leland was. We stopped in one of the "parks" to let the mule trains pass us. I began to know in my heart that Leland was lost, though I had no proof.

When we got to Beaver Lake, I knew Leland wasn't there. I felt my awareness go out around the lake and come back empty. The cowboys tried to tell me that he was probably off taking photos somewhere, or asleep under a tree. Herman confirmed that he had seen hiker tracks and dog tracks all the way up to Badger Pass. They busied themselves with setting up camp. I busied myself with setting up my tent and trying not to cry.

Dinnertime and still no Leland. By then I had figured out what had happened. By going over everything in my head and looking at the map again, I realized that it was possible to mistake one branch of the "Big River Trail" for another. That is, it was possible to head north on the Flathead River instead of north on Strawberry Creek. The trail was part of a big loop, but Leland wouldn't have known that without a map. Nobody else in camp believed me, but they knew the area well and it was a mistake they wouldn't have made. Nevertheless, Gregg took his horse and rode several miles around and down the Flathead side of the Big River Trail. He didn't know it then, but he had barely missed Leland in time and distance.

Not knowing that the two trails connected up north, Leland had finally figured out he'd taken a wrong turn and had turned around to head back. It got cold, as it usually does at higher altitudes at night. I put on my jacket and felt guilty because I was warm. Leland didn't have a jacket. I knew he had a lighter in his pocket and could start a fire. He'd have to stay up all night, but he'd survive.

I knew Leland would be hitting a wall soon, and he'd have no energy to go on. I tried really hard not to cry, but cried anyway. Herman took Sally's horse, Peso, and went to look for Leland down the Strawberry Creek Trail. I made a sack dinner for Leland, and Herman took it with him. I set up Leland's tent and put all of his and Tempest's stuff inside.

Long after nightfall, when I didn't see how it would be humanly possible for Herman to make it back through the bogs, we heard the soft sound of mud-muffled hooves. It was such a black night that we

A campfire burns above the Two Medicine River in the Lewis and Clark Range.

couldn't make out the horse and rider until they were about 10 feet away from us. Gregg got a flashlight and helped Herman with the horse. Herman took the dinner out of his saddlebags and handed it back to me. Oh, my brother.

Herman had ridden all the way back to our last camp and had seen absolutely no sign of Leland. I asked him how he made it through the bogs. "It was blackern' coal in there and I couldn't see a thing, so I just closed my eyes. That horse knows the way."

There was nothing more we could do. We went to our respective tents and sleeping bags. It started to rain. Oh, my brother. Every time the rain stopped, I slept a little. When the rain began again, I woke up and worried.

Everyone was scheduled to ride out the next morning except Leland and me. The plan was that I would wait there at Beaver Lake for Leland, with all my backpacking gear and all of his. If he didn't show up, I was to hang Leland's stuff in a tree using the anti-bear method we'd used all along, put my gear on my back and hike the twelve miles out to Swift Reservoir, where I'd find a Blackfeet Indian friend of Sally's and use his phone to call the Forest Service to have them search for Leland. I did not relish the prospect.

At first light, I was up and wandering around like a lost soul. Gregg and Herman drove the stock out to graze and I saw them pass through the fog in the dim light. The horses were running in a cloud on invisible hooves, their manes and tails a darker silver in the gray fog. The bell mare's bell sounded sad and bright at the same time. Where was my brother?

The sun slowly burned the fog off the lake and in the windless morning, every tree bore a bright burden of enormous wet drops, pendants of moisture shot through with light. At the last minute, Sally decided that Herman should stay with me. So Sally left me one cowboy, two horses, one mule, and some food. Herman was to bring me out if Leland didn't show up. We helped Gregg get his pack train loaded and they headed out. I knew I could take care of myself, but that it was safer and better to have Herman there. The silence was not as big.

Lake Levale in the Bob Marshall Wilderness is home to rare Arctic grayling fish.

Next to our campfire, we spread out one of the tattered pieces of canvas Herman uses to manny up a load for the mules. I was lying around with my boots off, reading bits of Emerson to keep me occupied, when Leland showed up. Herman just pointed off into the distance, and there were my brother and Tempest coming down the trail. Oh, my brother!

He really wasn't too badly off. He had walked more than thirty miles in a day-and-a-half. He felt stupid for making the mistake. Going off without food, water, and raingear was something he normally would not have done. Live and learn. I gave him some of the fried chicken that Sally had left me. Tempest got doggy food. It was too late to pack up and do anything more that day, so we all took a nap in the warm sunshine.

In the afternoon, Leland walked into the lake with his pants on and scrubbed the mud out of them. He changed his shirt, ate more food, and started looking good. But he said he just didn't have what it took to backpack another 30 miles to Marias Pass. We didn't have enough food to wait around for him to rest another day. Knowing when to quit is a skill that one develops over time. Most hikers can go home to recuperate after a week on the trail. If you are hiking long distances, you have to quit before some part of your body breaks down. We decided that we'd both go out with Herman the next morning.

The next day we took turns riding and walking. Even Herman walked, though he'd told me before, "I don't like walking much." He led the laden mule up the pass over Family Peak. The eastern side of the Front Range was quite dry, no more bogs, although there was plenty of water in the North Fork of Birch Creek as it made its way to the reservoir. There were even some impressive waterfalls, and a section of trail that looked down on the creek at such a steep angle that Herman said some of the hunters he guides get nervous there and won't look down. I rode Herman's horse and noted that I couldn't get it to walk as fast as Herman could in his sleep.

Two days later Leland and I were home. Horses are pastured in the field beyond my backyard, near my bedroom windows. In the middle of the night I heard them snorting and stomping and woke up. I sat up in my bed, thinking I was in my tent somewhere on the Divide. I thought, "I must have set up on high ground." It seemed that the ground fell away on either side of me. A deeper darkness led through what I took to be a hall of trees on my left. The horses spoke to each other in the night and I looked that way. The dim outline of a lampshade near the window finally brought me home, to my high bed. It started to rain. The horses always run and talk just before the rain. I went back to sleep on a wave of happiness.

We ended up hiking all of the CDT in Glacier National Park before we got back to the orphaned section of trail from Beaver Lake to Marias Pass. Our support crew helped us through Glacier in September, then Leland and I went back alone to fight the first snows of the season. At Muskrat Pass, we encountered more bogs, a fitting border marker for the end of the designated wilderness. We hiked around Running Owl Mountain, along Two Medicine River, and up Elkcalf Mountain, the names a reminder that we were near the Blackfeet Indian Nation. Bad weather played havoc with route-finding, so we just walked toward the sounds of the Burlington Northern trains and ended up at U.S. Highway 2.

We never strayed far from the ghosts of Lewis and Clark. They apparently named the pass after Lewis's cousin, Maria Wood. Blackfeet Indians called it "Backbone Pass." Marias Pass, at 5,216 feet above sea level, was the lowest pass over the Continental Divide that we crossed in Montana. I didn't feel like I'd been walking downhill, but I checked the maps, and the signs at the pass were correct. In the parking lot next to the highway, there were all kinds of mammoth stone sculptures for Theodore Roosevelt and other pioneers. The Summit Campground was closed, and black bear prints were visible on the human trails. Rangers close the campground early in September and turn off the water so the pipes won't freeze, but I was told that CDT hikers were welcome to cross the barriers and put up a tent there, and that water could be filtered out of the nearby stream.

The West Fork of the Sun River Valley is one of many areas in the Bob Marshall Wilderness that is frequented by grizzly bears. Red Butte shoulders into the sky on the horizon.

Marias Pass to the Canadian Border

▼▲▼

Glacier National Park, Designated and Alternate Routes, 145.4 miles

Since we began at Yellowstone National Park, my brother and I had hiked through sagebrush, juniper woodlands, grasslands, musky aspen groves, jail cells of lodgepole pines, dark worlds of Douglas-fir, avalanche chutes, and alpine tundra. We saw cliff faces thousands of feet high and forded icy rivers in shadowed canyons. What could Glacier National Park offer that we hadn't already seen?

The Continental Divide Trail in Glacier was like the rest of the trail on steroids. No hyperbole was too pumped up, all purple prose was justified. Glacier Park scenery was an echo of thunder in my soul. The sights sank me to my knees or rolled me over like a log going downriver. As you might imagine, this cramped my hiking style, but I enjoyed it.

But Glacier National Park came with a price. It was the only place for which we had to make reservations. The park was also where we had our most dangerous encounters with bears and our most bizarre confrontations with humankind. Our trek through Glacier National Park required a firm grasp of logistics, safety measures, diplomacy, and bureaucratic procedures.

A hiker pauses above Waterton Valley, south of the Canadian border.

Before we began, I called the land administrators and they sent me a raft of paperwork to fill out and rules to decipher. From Marias Pass to Many Glacier there was one CDT route through the park, but at Many Glacier the route split into a designated route and an alternate route. The designated CDT ended up in Waterton, Canada, and the alternate route ended at Chief Mountain Customs Station. We hiked both routes. I sent in reservation forms that cut the trek into segments that went from highway to highway. It cost more money that way, but it allowed us some flexibility, and the luxury of renewing our food supplies frequently.

We not only had our trusty support crew with us, but were joined by a motley crew of my other brothers. Robert came down from Alaska, Jerry from Boise, and Steve from Idaho Falls. I was the designated trip leader, but my brothers did not show me the respect that the office demanded. I got some revenge by being the only member of the party who hiked all the miles in Glacier National Park. Occasionally—all right, frequently—I reminded them of this fact.

For the first leg of our journey, the 15 miles from Marias Pass to the town of East Glacier Park, Robert joined Leland and me. Robert is from Alaska and can read bear sign and analyze terrain better than anyone.

Opposite: A spur trail from the Highline Trail, the designated route of the CDT, leads to Sue Lake near Fifty Mountain.

125

Along most of the park's trails, crews place seasonal bridges over watercourses, but not in this seldom-visited section. We climbed into and out of muddy gullies repeatedly, following cross-country ski markers that had been put up in the 1930s. We reached the highest point on this nearly flat section of trail near Summit Mountain. It was not impressive. No knock-your-socks-off scenery in this section.

Jerry and Steve joined Robert and me to hike the 10.5 miles from East Glacier Park to Two Medicine. I thought it was impossible to get lost on the Glacier trails, but a hiker from Australia was standing on the trail cursing his "stupid bloody map." Later we met some Americans who were lost about a mile from their lodgings. They had gotten turned around and were hiking away from the lodge. Must be fun to be a park ranger in such a place.

A tiger lily blooms in a subalpine forest west of Marias Pass.

We got our first dose of scenic overload from, appropriately enough, Scenic Point. Rising Wolf Mountain, big enough to be two mountains and red all over, towered over Two Medicine Lake and dwarfed the ranger station with its toy flag. At the limit of our view to the west was Pumpelly Pillar. I wanted to climb them all, to explore everything. For a reality check, I looked to the southeast, where I could see the northern end of the Bob Marshall Wilderness, from which we had so recently escaped. My eyes always want to see more than my legs can deliver.

From Scenic Point to Two Medicine, we hiked in a merciless gale. We were almost reduced to crawling to keep the wind from blowing us off the cliffs. We found one niche of rock to rest in and stopped there, panting, while the wind roared over us. Still, at the end of the day some wider spirit roamed inside me as if I'd caught the wind, the mountains, and the long views and held them inside my skin.

We got a taste of the unpredictability of hiking itineraries for Glacier Park when we checked in at the Two Medicine Ranger Station. One of the campgrounds we had selected was closed because of grizzly bear activity. We reorganized the hike to include Oldman Lake instead. Hikers are required to watch an instructional video before receiving a backcountry permit. "Our trip leader will watch the video," my

Fall arrives on the Autumn Creek Trail in Glacier National Park.

The Appistoki Falls surge between Scenic Point and Two Medicine Lake in Glacier National Park.

brothers said, and left. The video told me that it would be a rare privilege to see a bear.

After watching videos, filing forms, and attaching license-to-hike tags to my backpack, we departed. The trail wound its way up the narrow valley of the Dry Fork, climbing steadily between glaciated peaks. The red and plum colors that dominate the high terrain here are mostly the result of iron oxide, the same pigment found in everything from house paint to fingernail polish. The green color also derives from iron, but resulted from a reductive process combining iron with silica in the absence of oxygen, creating chlorite.

All right, I can hear a few readers groaning (along with my brothers) but I find all the geology and chemistry endlessly interesting. So if you just find it endless, skip those parts. The hike to Oldman Lake was breathtaking, even without my educational background noise.

A spur trail led 0.3 mile to Oldman Lake. My brothers complained that, as team leader, I should have informed them of the extra 0.3 mile they would have to hike. Help me, Lord. Packs were doffed and three "old men" lay on the shore soaking up the sun and the sights. A host of butterflies lit on Jerry.

At dinner, we shared the "food preparation area" with other hikers. Some of them managed to pack a lot of cooking gear and ingredients for three-course meals. One guy showed up with a propane bottle two feet high. His wife announced, "That pass just about kicked my ass, but I still got some left." She turned her ass our way and we confirmed that she had some left. The couple with the three-course meal asked if we had "done The Bob"— and then my cover was blown. It came out that I had indeed done The Bob and just about everything else. In further conversation, I did not show sufficient disgust for the horses in The Bob and was downgraded from hail-fellow-well-met to ignorant destroyer of the planet.

We concluded our socializing, and got our food bags ready to hang. The park provides hanging poles at each campsite, but no rope. Jerry said he was going to hoist himself up there so he wouldn't have to worry about the bears. We figured out how to do it, but he chickened out. Back at the tent site, we discovered that Steve still had a chocolate bar the size of a small pillow in his pack. Back to the food bags. To

Wooden bridges lead hikers across the many-tiered Virginia Falls.

get to the food bags we had to pass the food prep area again, so this was getting to be quite entertaining for the other campers.

A pretty and friendly woman told me that her husband carried all their food, but was still hiking faster than she liked, so she just kept adding to his pack until he slowed down to her speed. I looked at her husband and he just nodded. He was just about the buffest thing I had seen on the trail. "I need one of those," I thought. "Do we have to hang up our toothpaste, too?" the woman asked. I assured her that she should put all her smelly toiletries out of reach of bears. "Toothpaste," Jerry said. Back to the tent site. Back to the food bags.

Oldman Lake weather report: The sun disappeared, the clouds rolled in. It rained, lightning filled the sky, winds ripped at our tent stakes, and thunder loudly boomed and ricocheted off of the cliff walls.

The next morning, as we climbed to Pitamakan Pass, a round break in the clouds allowed the sun to spotlight the cliffs above the lake, the light moving until it came to rest on a band of grazing bighorn sheep. We stood around and looked at all the splendor while Robert changed into cooler hiking pants, briefly flashing his skivvies at the sheep.

Glacier National Park must hold a Ph.D. in the science of cutting trails. The switchbacks are perfectly graded to get you up and down without causing erosion and without excessive wandering around. Going over the top was a breeze and none of us got our asses kicked, though we found the poetic "that pass just about kicked my ass" worth repeating.

As we descended from Pitamakan Pass, we came across the rototilling efforts of grizzly bears. Two-hundred-pound boulders had been casually tossed aside. The trail escaped harm because its packed earth was not conducive to rodent tunnels.

We lost count of the number of waterfalls we saw on this trek. I thought back to how excited I'd been to find one waterfall in the Scapegoat Wilderness, and to how often we'd had trouble finding water along the CDT. Glacier National Park was another world entirely, one filled with the voices of water.

We stopped at Atlantic Creek Campground, one of the worst for crowding hikers close together on small sites. The food preparation area was also cramped. After camping wherever we pleased month after month, it was a considerable hardship to fit ourselves into such tight confines.

The Saint Mary Piedmont Glacier was more than 1,200 feet thick before it began to melt about 13,000 years ago. The Saint Mary Falls, pictured here, is a remnant of that land-scouring giant.

We got an early start on the trail to Triple Divide Pass. The pass is a geological marvel. Educational geology warning: Waters from this pass drain indirectly to the Pacific Ocean, the Atlantic Ocean, and Hudson Bay. Yes—that's right—Hudson Bay, and thence to the Arctic Ocean.

We stopped to read a "trail closed" sign at the spur trail to Medicine Grizzly Lake. In addition to text, there was a grizzly icon. A quarter-mile up the trail we had a tense encounter with a grizzly sow and cub. I guess they didn't see the signs, they were out of the closed area. The sow was rolling across the tundra like a furry locomotive, the cub trailing behind. Strong winds blew our voices away from the bears so they didn't hear us coming. A surprised bear is a dangerous bear. We had no place to go except off a cliff, so we stood there foolishly, trying to look non-combative. Robert talked in a monotone, the idea being that we were not a male grizzly and therefore not a threat. The bear stood to sniff and take a look. Jerry told her we were old and stringy, not good eating. She ambled on, moving toward Atlantic Creek Campground, where our campmates were still cooking breakfast. We wished them well and breathed a sigh of relief. Jerry took the last-in-line position to watch our backtrail.

When we arrived at Red Eagle Lake to camp, two rangers met us and greeted us with, "Well, I see you made it out alive." The rangers were armed with gigantic pepper spray canisters. Having confirmed our status as live hikers, the rangers departed.

Because we were alone at the foot of Red Eagle Lake, we briefly indulged in a no-no and tested the reality of the landscape with operatic shouts. The echoes came back quickly from the near mountains, arrived more slowly from the next ring, and slower still from the third ring of mountains. These concentric rings of echoes were like an ultrasound of the surrounding geography, touching the mountains and receiving a response.

Educational geology warning: Red Eagle Mountain is a big lump of red argillite, a clay-rich sedimentary rock that formed from billion-year-old mud. The outlet from Red Eagle Lake is a rough, white-water spume over a sill of hard rock that formed a natural dam. We had already seen emerald-green and turquoise water, but this stream was aquamarine, as clear as a gem.

As we hiked out the next morning, we noted fresh black bear prints overlaying the prints of the rangers. Closer to Saint Mary Lake, we saw wolf scat on the trail. So far, we were all still alive, but Steve was flagging. Unconsciously, I had increased my hiking speed thanks to thoughts of dinner at Mom's Mobile Wilderness Cafe.

An unnamed waterfall flows on Reynolds Creek near the Piegan Pass Trailhead in Glacier National Park.

From Piegan Pass hikers can view portions of "The Garden Wall," the most well-known arête in Glacier National Park.

Steve was about 100 yards behind when Robert called out that we should rest. We made it to the lakeshore before Steve turned an interesting shade of green and keeled over. I felt terrible. My first thought was that I had pushed too hard. We sat for a while and waited for Steve to recover, but after tossing his cookies, he was too weak to lift his backpack. Robert stayed with Steve, setting up a sleeping pad and sleeping bag to keep him warm. We couldn't find anything else wrong with him, apart from being weak and green. Jerry and I put our packs on and force-marched out of there at top hiking speed. We could have gone faster without our packs, but I nixed that idea. If something happened to one of us, we would need the first aid and other survival gear we carried. I was glad there were four of us. It is never a good idea to hike alone in bear country.

We were almost to Virginia Falls when we met Dad and Leland out on a photo expedition. I was really glad to see them. With Dad's truck nearby we would save a lot of time arranging a rescue for Steve. Together we headed for the Going-to-the-Sun Road.

I could smell the tourists before we saw them. Visitors streamed down the wide path, tennis-shoe-shod and perfumed with a dizzying array of chemicals, including the suffocating laundry soaps meant to imitate springtime in the mountains or fresh lemons. I wanted a gas mask. My nose had apparently undergone a rebirth of sorts. I wondered

A marmot, resident of alpine terrain, investigates the camera.

what grizzly bears thought of this cornucopia of overpowering smells. I would guess that, for bears, it bore a strong resemblance to yummy garbage. We plowed through the tourist hordes, and I suppose we didn't smell good to them either.

After what seemed like an interminable wait, the park rangers showed up with a medic and the keys to one of their fast boats. Steve and Robert got a lovely ride across the lake, and Jerry and I were jealous. Steve was subjected to a medical exam, and the nurse asked him if he had been drinking. There was a long pause while Steve and I raised our eyebrows and refrained from comment. Then we figured it out, "Oh, you mean water." None of us were dehydrated, including Steve. We never did find out what was wrong with him. He said he was having a good time right up until the moment that he keeled over.

At Rising Sun Campground, Steve set up his tent and rested. The rest of us worked on our backpacks for the next expedition. After we left to hike the Piegan Pass Trail and the support crew moved to Many Glacier, a camper was mauled through his tent at Rising Sun Campground. Firearms are not allowed in the park, so we purchased another large can of pepper spray. We carried two on every hike.

Leland, Robert, and I day-hiked from Saint Mary Lake to Many Glacier, crossing over Piegan Pass, which still held pockets of old snow from the previous season. "Piegan" is the language of the Blood Indians, a branch of the Blackfeet.

Robert had a good time reading bear sign and bear trails. A grizzly had obviously been stalking the mountain goats that watched us from green ledges that hung on the gray cliffs. This was the trail that Vice President Al Gore hiked when he posed for a photo op at Grinnell Glacier. Gore traveled with some armed security guards. We should all have such a luxury! Parts of the trail were signed as a "Grizzly Frequenting Area."

Of all the beautiful waterfalls we saw in the park, this 15.6-mile section of trail offered the best of the best. Morning Eagle Falls was a broad beauty, flowing over a rock face below Piegan Pass. On the "Garden Wall," an arête west of Morning Eagle, were seven more nameless waterfalls. In September, snowdrifts from the past season still hugged the wall. Pelting waterfalls drilled semicircles into the drifts,

The Granite Park Chalet on the Highline Trail in Glacier National Park.

creating blue, icy caves behind them. At Feather Plume Falls, water plunged down the face of the rocks, and launched into a long free-fall where the rock was undercut. Wind picked up most of the water before it hit the ground, sending a cloud of vapor into the air. At Grinnell Lake multiple waterfalls came down off the cliff—some of them were really huge—tons of water pouring down into the silt-green lake. Hidden Falls, a short jaunt off the trail, was actually two falls of white water in a moss-covered gorge.

The Garden Wall was truly enchanting in its own right. A light dusting of snow accented the serrated edge of the arête, and gauzy mists alternately revealed and concealed the battlements. The effect was too austere to be called beautiful, but so impressively moody that I wanted to lie on my back and look up at it all day. So I did for about five minutes, listening to the sounds of elk bugling and water falling.

Morning Eagle Falls and Cataract Creek are visible below Piegan Pass in Glacier National Park.

Near Swiftcurrent Lake, with Leland in the lead and hiking fast, we rounded a corner and came face to face with a mama black bear and two cubs. We had been talking loudly, but the bears were not fazed in the least. "Whoa," Leland said, and had his pepper spray out and the safety off in a nanosecond. We backed up slowly. The bears sauntered toward us. We backed up some more and the bears kept coming. A trail crew came up behind us and we all left the trail, going down to a boat dock on the lake. The bears calmly continued on the human trail until they came to what must have been their accustomed bear trail and exited. It was Miller Time for the trail crew, so they hastened on down the trail toward the ranger station, shouting "Hey bear!" and clapping their hands.

At Many Glacier, we chose to hike the designated CDT first, climbing to Swiftcurrent Pass and then following the Highline and Waterton Valley trails to Canada. My brother

The midsection of Virginia Falls surges near where Virginia Creek empties into Saint Mary Lake.

Robert commented on how much the terrain looked like Alaska. More than one-third of Glacier National Park is alpine, with sheer cliffs, talus slopes, snowfields, and glaciers. The elevations are not that high, but glaciation, a northern latitude, and the strong visual impact of mountains rising over low plains makes 8,000-foot mountains look like giants.

We met two German tourists who were white as new-washed sheets and quaking like aspen leaves. In fractured English, they told a tale of meeting four grizzly bears. They were so distraught that they couldn't tell us where they had left their backpacks. We escorted them to Granite Park Chalet. Night was coming on fast as we made our wary way to warn the other campers in the nearby backcountry campsite. Deer crashed around in the brush near the trail; they didn't know where to go with the bear scent on one side and human traffic on the other.

In response to the bear sighting, the other campers said, "Cool, let's go see them." NOT a good idea. We decided to spend the night in the chalet. The Granite Park Chalet harbored the smell of its past and the decay of its present. It was like a huge wooden sounding board, amplifying footsteps and voices. In the early 1900s tourists came up on mules and horses, stayed in the lodge, and threw raw meat off the balcony to attract bears. Ignorance is the mother of stupidity, but they also had guns, lots of guns. Now everything is kept cleaner to discourage bears, but the meadows below the lodge are still locally known as "Mauling Meadows," a name you won't find on your map. I didn't like the ghoulish humor or the euphemisms like "bear encounter" for the times when a human died or was mauled near the chalet.

We got up at first light, and Leland shot photos instead of bears from the balcony. North of Granite Park Chalet, the geographical Divide leaves the Lewis and Clark Mountains, crosses West Flattop, and turns north to follow the Livingston Range. The trail takes a saner route, east of all those glaciers.

When we pulled into the Fifty Mountain Campground, some younger hikers muttered, "Looks like a bunch of old farts." The food preparation area was humming with backpackers and conversations about gear and blister remedies. After doctoring several blisters and giving out advice, we were upgraded to "veterans." I didn't say anything, but noted that we were the only ones who weren't limping or injured in some way. I thought about the many miles of trail that had brought me this far north and decided I was proud to be either a veteran or old fart.

Jerry mentally divided the campsite into a grid and counted the "Do-Not" signs. There was a sign for every two square feet of "barren core." Between the signs the tents were so close together that, when Robert started to snore that night, I hit Jerry. The snoring didn't stop, so I hit him again. "That's not me—it's Robert!"

LOGAN PASS

Logan Pass, "the Crown of the Continent," is west of the route of the CDT, on the Going-to-the-Sun Road. The visitors' center is full of displays that feature the history, flora, and fauna of Glacier National Park. A trail that begins as a boardwalk near the visitors' center leads southwest to Hidden Lake. This is the shortest route to Glacier's high country near Bearhat Mountain. North of the highway, the Highline Trail begins, offering a day hike to Granite Park Chalet and Swiftcurrent Pass. When Piegan Pass is snowed in, this route serves as an alternate access point to the Continental Divide Trail.

GEOLOGY

The mountains of Glacier National Park seem to stand still in time. Certainly, they don't change much in the lifetime of one Continental Divide Trail hiker, but the changes of the past can be read in the rocks. The 200-million-year-old layer cake of the park's geology is a composite of rock that formed from sediments first laid down in a shallow sea or lake about 1.5 billion years ago. The sediments eroded from granite that cooled 1.7 billion years ago. There is no other granite in North America of such ancient lineage—its closest match in terms of time comes from Australia. The park's mountains probably had their start thousands of miles from where they ended up, carried by continental drift to a collision with another tectonic plate. The change was slow, about an inch a year by most accounts, but inexorable.

From Fifty Mountain it was all downhill to Waterton Lake. The highest point on the trail was 7,420 feet and we camped at Goat Haunt, on Waterton Lake, at 4,200 feet, our lowest elevation since we began. On our way down we saw several bear trails, claw marks on trees, and bear scat so fresh that we had to slow down and give the bear time to get off the trail.

Rangers at Goat Haunt said a grizzly had been nosing around, and advised us to put our food in a restroom closet. We decided it was more sanitary to hang the bags from a tree and were doing so when a backcountry ranger showed up. She had been called in to discipline us. Her worry was that we wouldn't be able to hang the food bags because there was no official food-hanging pole. She tried again to get us to put the food in the dirty closet, then watched us hang the bags. Satisfied that we weren't entirely incompetent, she sat down for a little conversation. We praised the trails and the scenery in the park, but said the tent sites and food prep areas were small. She said they had all been measured and were "roomy," and that creating any more barren core would be a crime.

Here are my tips for hikers who live in the real world: Four people cannot comfortably fit in most of Glacier's tent sites. If you have the money to do so, reserve a site for every two people. Bring a good groundcloth because most of the sites are rocky and wet, built like a shallow bathtub. If you love to socialize, you'll like the food prep areas; if not, bring food that's quick to fix and schedule your meals earlier than normal.

Wildflowers creep along the rocky alpine slopes of the Highline Trail.
Flattop Mountain and Livingstone Range are visible in the distance.

Another ranger/customs official came by and said to help ourselves to the open-air fireplace and the cut wood. It was great to have a fire, and to sit in comfort by the lake. We watched the sunset and got up to watch the sunrise over the lake the next morning. The sun rose, there was a rainbow over the lake, we could hear a wolf howling in the distance, and the back-country ranger showed up with a wheelbarrow full of tools to put up a food-hanging pole.

From Goat Haunt, there is an 8.7-mile trail to Waterton Townsite, or hikers can catch the boat that runs twice a day. Crossing the international boundary was anticlimactic. It looked like an old bulldozer had cut through the trees because an old bulldozer *had* cut through the trees. Arriving at a real Canadian town with chocolate shops and restaurants galore, however, was truly exciting. There is only one animal on the trails that gets hungrier than a grizzly, and that's a backpacker.

So, we had arrived at long last in Canada. I would have liked to celebrate, but we weren't done hiking yet. Leland and I had to go back and hike the alternate route. My other brothers had wisely given up and were ready to take it easy for a while.

The alternate route was as scenic as the designated route. And it was shorter. We hiked it in two days and were back in camp in time for dinner. Except for the steep climb over Redgap Pass, the trail consisted mostly of gentle grades and few switchbacks. Park officials gave us an "elevation alert" for the 2,000-foot ascent and the 2,800-foot descent. There was the usual grizzly bear warning, and also a warning about slippery rocks where water crosses the trail. Seems that hikers had been

stopping to filter water and then slipping over the edge, catapulting down waterfalls and dying on the rocks below. Of course, the trail was much safer than many others we had negotiated in the past, and the elevation gain was 1,000 feet less than what we'd experienced at Targhee Pass, and no rangers had supervised our bear-avoidance procedures for the previous 800 miles. All the babysitting felt decidedly strange, but I understand the reason for it, and I admire the park's ability to handle so many visitors with relative grace.

The Kintla formation stone of Redgap Pass was truly red, especially when wet. Even in light snow, the views from the pass were spellbinding, but we couldn't stop to admire them. Leland passed me half an energy bar as we climbed because it was too cold and windy to risk a lunch break. It was now late September and trail crews were removing the seasonal bridges. Luckily, we were hiking ahead of them. The Belly River was big and bold, dangerous to ford in cold weather.

We camped at Elizabeth Lake and it was brutal. The wind blew both water and snow into the food prep area, so we set up our stove in the lee of a tree about two feet outside of the area, but on the barren core of the trail. A group of hikers showed up and one of them pointed at us and said, "Thou Shalt Not." They also told us there was no use stopping at a campground where campfires were allowed because "there's no dry wood, so you can't start a fire anyway." Leland and I just looked at each other. We could start a fire in even the wettest conditions.

In the morning we left without further offending anyone. Dawn Mist Falls and the meadow at the Belly River Ranger Station were photo-worthy,

The author admires the view below Dawn Mist Falls on the Belly River, located in Glacier National Park.

> *"There is only one animal on the trails that gets hungrier than a grizzly, and that's a backpacker"*

though we had to hurry a bit because the storm followed us down river. I wanted to linger because the aspen trees were spending their gold in the wind.

At the Chief Mountain Customs Station, I illegally put one foot into Canada and then we hitchhiked back to the support crew. Dad treated me to tokens for a hot shower at the Swiftcurrent Inn. I can't think why.

GLACIER NATIONAL PARK AND THE BLACKFEET INDIAN NATION

To obtain a copy of Glacier National Park's Backcountry Camping Policies, call (406) 888-7800; or write to Glacier National Park, National Park Service, P. O. Box 128, West Glacier, MT 59936; or visit the website: www.nps.gov/glac.

The Continental Divide Trail crosses about five miles of Blackfeet Tribal Lands near East Glacier Park, on the Autumn Creek and Scenic Point trails. A $5 permit, available at most East Glacier Park shops, is required for all recreational uses, including backpacking. For further information, contact Blackfeet Fish & Wildlife at 406-338-7207.

Swiftcurrent Ridge Lake mirrors a stormy sky in Glacier National Park.

APPENDIX A: BIBLIOGRAPHY AND SUGGESTED READING

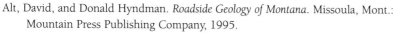

Alt, David, and Donald Hyndman. *Roadside Geology of Montana*. Missoula, Mont.: Mountain Press Publishing Company, 1995.

Back, Joe. *Horses, Hitches and Rocky Trails*. Boulder, Colo.: Johnson Printing Company, 1997.

Bergon, Frank. *The Journals of Lewis & Clark*. New York: Penguin Books, 1989.

Boone, Lalia. *Idaho Place Names: A Geographical Dictionary*. Moscow, Idaho: University of Idaho Press, 1988.

Cheek, Roland. *Learning to Talk Bear*. Great Falls, Mont.: Northwinds Publishing and Printing, 1997.

Conley, Cort. *Idaho for the Curious*. Cambridge, Idaho: Backeddy Books, 1982.

Craighead, John; Frank Craighead; and Ray Davis. *A Field Guide to Rocky Mountain Wildflowers*. New York: New York Public Library and Stonesong Press, Inc., 1993.

Florin, Lambert. *Ghost Towns of the West*. New York: Superior Publishing Company, 1971.

Garcia, Andrew. *Tough Trip Through Paradise*. San Francisco: Rock Foundation, Comstock Editions, 1967.

Jones, Tom Lorang. *Colorado's Continental Divide Trail: The Official Guide*. Englewood, Colo.: Westcliffe Publishers, Inc., 1997.

Lopez, Tom. *Exploring Idaho's Mountains*. Seattle: The Mountaineers, 1990.

Maley, Terry. *Exploring Idaho Geology*. Boise, Idaho: Mineral Land Publications, 1987.

Murie, Olaus. *Animal Tracks*. New York: Houghton Mifflin Company, 1974.

Rockwell, David. *Glacier National Park, A Natural History Guide*. Boston: Houghton Mifflin Company, 1995.

Taylor, Ronald. *Sagebrush Country*. Missoula, Mont.: Mountain Press Publishing Company, 1992.

Thomas, David; Jay Miller; Richard White; Peter Nabokov; and Phillip Deloria. *The Native Americans: An Illustrated History*. Atlanta: Turner Publishing, 1993.

Tirrel, Norma. *Montana, Compass American Guides*. Oakland, Calif.: Fodor's Travel Publications, Inc., 1997.

Ward, Geoffrey. *The West: An Illustrated History*. New York: Little, Brown, and Co., 1996.

Whitney, Stephen, et al. *Western Forests: The Audubon Society Nature Guides*. New York: Alfred A. Knopf, 1990.

APPENDIX B: CONSERVATION AND TRAIL ADVOCACY GROUPS

Adventure Cycling Association
P.O. Box 8308
Missoula, MT 59807
(800) 755-2453
Web: www.adv-cycling.org

Alliance of the Wild Rockies
415 N. Higgins Ave.
Missoula, MT 59802
(406) 721-5420

Backcountry Horsemen of America
P.O. Box 5431
Helena, MT 59604
E-mail: hlazym@tcc-cmc.net
Web: www.3rivers.net/~gullicph/mt.html

Bob Marshall Foundation
P.O. Box 1052
Kalispell, MT 59903
(406) 758-5237
Web: www.bobmarshall.org

Continental Divide Trail Alliance
P.O. Box 628
Pine, CO 80470
(888) 909-CDTA
E-mail: cdnst@aol.com
Web: www.cdtrail.org

Continental Divide Trail Society
3704 N. Charles St., #601
Baltimore, MD 21218
(410) 235-9610
E-mail: cdtsociety@aol.com
Web: www.gorp.com/cdts/

Glacier National Park Associates
P.O. Box 91
Kalispell, MT 59903
(406) 888-5241
Web: www.nps.gov/glac/gnpa.htm

The Glacier National Park History Association
P.O. Box 428
West Glacier, MT 59936
(406) 888-5756
Web: www.nps.gov/glac/gnha1.htm

Leave No Trace
P.O. Box 997
Boulder, CO 80305
Web: www.lnt.org

Montana Wilderness Association
P.O. Box 635
Helena, MT 59624
(406) 443-7350

Save the Chalets
704 Birch St.
Helena, MT 59601-9923
(888) CHALET1
Web: www.nps.gov/glac/chalets.htm

History of the Continental Divide National Scenic Trail

The Continental Divide National Scenic Trail (CDNST) began in 1966 as the dream of Benton MacKaye, an 87-year-old man who had already devoted much of his life to seeing the Appalachian Trail come to fruition. MacKaye's idea was to create a trail that would connect a series of wilderness areas along the Divide from Montana's border with Canada to New Mexico's border with Mexico.

MacKaye (rhymes with "deny") proposed his idea to Congress, which soon authorized a study of the trail under the National Trails Act of 1968. At around the same time, a Baltimore attorney by the name of Jim Wolf was hiking the 2,000-mile-long Appalachian Trail, which he completed in 1971. Inspired to seek out a new hiking challenge further afield, Wolf walked the Divide Trail from the Canadian border to Rogers Pass, Montana, in 1973. He soon published a guidebook covering that section of the trail and devoted much of his time to advocating its official designation. After a 1976 study by the Bureau of Outdoor Recreation found the scenic quality of the trail to surpass anything available anywhere else in the country, the Congressional Oversight Committee of the National Trail System held hearings on the trail in 1978, at which Wolf testified. The CDNST received official recognition from Congress later that year under the National Parks and Recreation Act.

In that same year, Wolf founded the Continental Divide Trail Society (CDTS) to garner publicity for the trail and involve the public in work surrounding its construction, particularly its route selection. Wolf continued to hike portions of the trail each summer, and by the mid-'80s he had completed all of its 3,100 miles.

The United States Forest Service is responsible for managing most of the land through which the trail passes. In the 1980s, its work on the trail progressed at different rates in different areas, but it suffered in general from a lack of public involvement. In 1994, two trail advocates began working under the auspices of a group called the Fausel Foundation to raise funds and build support for the trail. By 1995, their efforts evolved into the Continental Divide Trail Alliance (CDTA), a nonprofit organization devoted to fund-raising, publicity, education about the trail, and grassroots volunteer coordination. The CDTA founders were Bruce Ward, formerly the president of the American Hiking Society, and his wife, Paula, a landscape architect.

In its first year, the CDTA grew to include 425 individuals or families, 20 corporate sponsors, and a budget of $400,000. Estimates suggest the Alliance coordinated volunteer work worth $70,000 in that first year. However, trail advocates are quick to point out that there is much work yet to be done. Completion and maintenance of the trail will require funding and volunteer coordination throughout the 21st century.

Generously contributed by Tom Lorang Jones
Revised from *Colorado's Continental Divide Trail: The Official Guide*

The Continental Divide Trail Alliance
Protecting a Vital National Resource

How can you help?
By becoming a member of the Continental Divide Trail Alliance (CDTA). Your willingness to join thousands of concerned citizens across the country will make the difference. Together, we can provide the financial resources needed to complete the trail.

The CDTA is a nonprofit membership organization formed to help protect, build, maintain, and manage the CDT. The CDTA serves a broad-based constituency and includes people who enjoy recreating on public lands, as well as those concerned about overdevelopment.

As a CDTA member, you will:

- Protect a vital and precious natural resource
- Ensure trail maintenance and completion
- Improve trail access
- Support informational and educational programs
- Champion volunteer projects
- Advocate for policy issues that support the CDT

What does it take to help us? Just one cent a mile.
We realize there are a lot of demands on your time and budget. That's why we're only asking you to give a little—just one cent a mile to support the Trail. For a modest membership fee of $31, you will help us go so very far, and finish what was courageously started so long ago.

For more information
or to send your contribution, write to:

Continental Divide Trail Alliance
P.O. Box 628
Pine, CO 80470
(303) 838-3760
www.cdtrail.org

Please make checks payable to CDTA

AFTERWORD

The simple act of putting one foot in front of the other for almost 1,000 miles lends perspective to life and tunes your "bull" detector so you can get back to what's important. We hike to see if the wind is blowing, or if the moon is full. It is like waking up from a long sleep.

People who already live this way don't see what all the fuss is about. You know the ones—they have a look in their eyes of always seeing a far horizon while the rest of us only vaguely know that we have lost something. These seers of the simpler truths might think you pretty stupid for strapping a backpack on and suffering on the roof of the continent, but some of us have to work that hard to finally come back to ourselves.

A human being is a nexus, a place and a space where everything comes together and nature can speak. We have an inborn instinct, commensurate with Native American legends, that the highest mountains rise up into an otherwise unattainable promised land. What could be a better realization of our role in this world than to hike along the spine of all the tall mountains and speak their truths? It is a measure of its significance that the idea of a Continental Divide National Scenic Trail has held a great deal of appeal since it was first proposed. The trail is still not complete, but the idea is faultless.

Straight Creek, pictured here in autumn, carries enough water in spring to make crossing it a dangerous proposition.

Several mountain ranges are visible from the valley where I live, and I know them like friends. They are difficult friends, hard to get along with, apt to turn nasty without warning, just as apt to surprise me with a sudden insight or with beauties small and large. They are particularly hard on my feet, offering the soreness, blisters, turned ankles, and just plain fatigue of rough terrain.

If nothing else, when I get off the trail, I appreciate what I have at home. Running water, a roof that doesn't leak when it rains, a sit-down toilet, a soft bed. The smallest luxuries suddenly seem magical and extravagant. They *are* miraculous, and without trying, I find myself making do with a lot less of them. Every small thing is such a joy that I don't need so much. I go out for a walk and I have to stop, struck by the wonder of it all. "Wow, look at that! How broad and flat and smooth it is!" My feet rejoice in the sidewalk. Contrast is a great teacher.

—*Lynna Howard*
Alias, PrueHeart the Wanderer